C000192589

THE SMILE OF GOD

michael

may God smile

on you always.

Janet

Feb '06

As ever to Michele, Sam and Beth – I love you all more than ever and know that my life would be infinitely poorer without you guys.

THE SMILE OF GOD

Andy Hawthorne

survivor

First published 2005

ISBN 1 84291 236 4

Survivor is an imprint of
KINGSWAY COMMUNICATIONS LTD
Lottbridge Drove, Eastbourne BN23 6NT, England.
Email: books@kingsway.co.uk
Printed in Canada

CONTENTS

ACKNOWLEDGEMENTS

Once again, thanks to all the heroes at The Message who have faithfully stood with, prayed, given and served, so that this vision could move forward. You know who you are.

Thanks also to Craig Borlase for sorting out my manuscript and to Richard Herkes and Les Moir at Survivor for believing in this book in the first place and for lots of wisdom and support along the way.

Hezekiah trusted in the Lord, the God of Israel. There was no-one like him among all the kings of Judah, either before him or after him. He held fast to the Lord and did not cease to follow him; he kept the commands the Lord had given Moses. And the Lord was with him; he was successful in whatever he undertook. (2 Kings 18:5–7)

INTRODUCTION

Of all the names of all the bands in all the world, 'The Sheep' must be one of the most dodgy. I met them once. The slightly ageing American rockers were all ex-drugged-up hippies, and they turned up at our local youth group. I was twelve, and naturally thought they were fantastic. I also thought the message they brought was pretty cool. So when, at the end of the concert, one of the band invited anyone who wanted to join them to become a Christian, I knew it was for me. I was in.

Things carried on going well for a while, and I

worked hard at my faith for the next six months. But, slowly, like so many teenagers, I started to compromise. Within a year, very few people at Moseley Hall Boys School would have guessed I was a Christian. I'd put more time into my routine than my faith: clowning around; smoking; drinking, and trying to cop off with the girls from the school across the road. Study the word of God? What a joke.

Things are different for me now, but I still remember the challenges I faced back then. Even though I've been able to meet some amazing men and women of God over the last few years – the kind of people who have done incredible things in his service – I've got to admit that the person I respect the most is someone who, at 14 or 15 years old, consistently stands up for Jesus. The school environment might be hostile, and there might be huge pressures to fit in and compromise, but they are standing strong and keeping the faith. One thing is for sure: I couldn't do it.

It wasn't until I was 17 and had left school that I started to get serious about my faith. It was all because of my brother, Simon. He'd been radically converted and had me fully on his radar. There was no way that he was going to let me get away with not coming back to God.

I can clearly remember the night when it happened. I'd listened from the pews of our local church while Simon had given his testimony. On my way home, I realised that I had to do something about what I'd heard. So that night, I knelt at my bedside and prayed what was actually a rather stupid prayer: 'Lord, I'm so sorry I messed up. But if you will have me back, this is it. I really want to go for it and live all out for you.'

Stupid? Absolutely. God specialises in having idiots like Andy Hawthorne back; throughout history, he's taken repentant rebels like me and forgiven them, starting to use them for his amazing eternal purposes. There are no ifs or buts about it.

It didn't take long for me to know that he'd accepted me back and filled me with his Spirit. I didn't get angelic visitations and I didn't start speaking in tongues, but I knew all right. First, I had an amazing joy and excitement about my faith. Then, I sensed a massive passion, a real desire to get out and tell other people about it; that was when God gave me something of the heart and gift of being an evangelist. To be honest, I've been living off it ever since, and it has kept me going. During the whole time that we've ducked and dived with our various attempts to make Jesus known in Manchester, that one night in 1977 has been the backbone, the foundation on which the rest has been built.

Of course, since then the attempts that my mates and I made at evangelism have had varying degrees of success. I remember our early strategies involved going around the local pubs trying to engage the drunkards in a little bit of God-chat. While they weren't looking, we'd surreptitiously swap their Watney's Red Barrel beer-mats for ones that said: 'Come to your local . . .' on one side and on the other: '. . . church'. It was all very cheesy but I think it might have made God smile a little.

Since then, we've done loads of mission stuff in Manchester and seen God change the lives of thousands of people. In the process, there have been millions of pounds raised – often in the most nerve-racking ways possible. I absolutely know that the gospel is true and that it works like nothing else. So this is good. I should be happy, right? But after all these years, I'm left with the slightly frustrating questions that I'm sure many of you can relate to: Why haven't we seen more? Just what will it take to get to the place where we are not just seeing good things happen but where whole communities are utterly transformed, cities are changed and a nation turns back to God? How do we get God's smile to break out all over the place? What do we need to do to see our half-baked plans and good intentions turned into something that truly reflects God's almighty glory?

This book is written in the sure knowledge that all these things really can happen: we really can expect to see big changes, to watch in amazement as God ramps up the power and transforms a nation; all that amazing stuff God is doing around the world can be done right here too.

Of course, that can only happen when God

says so, and, yes, it's true that real revival is a totally sovereign work of God, the kind that depends on him far more than on us. It's down to him when he chooses to accelerate his amazing eternal salvation plan, but I've become equally convinced that we've got a part to play in it too. I think that our prayers and obedience might be all that it takes to influence great moves of God. You want proof? Take a look at a young king called Hezekiah. Almost 3,000 years ago, he and his people knew the smile of God: the Lord was with them and they were successful in whatever they undertook (see 2 Kings 18:7).

God was also with John Wesley. Two hundred years ago, Britain was morally in a big mess. Like today, there were people caught up in all sorts of sin, and the churches were emptying fast. It was then that Britain's last great national revival hit. On the back of it, around 50 per cent of the population decided they wanted to join a church. And these weren't just pew-warmers, but fired-up Christians intent on pushing forwards incredible social reform. Ministries to the poor were springing up all across the nation. The church was right at the heart of education and welfare reform, and it even spearheaded the abolition of slavery. Reliable historians have claimed that if it hadn't been for the Wesleyan revival the UK would have descended into civil war. However, despite seeing literally millions converted, John Wesley himself said, 'Give me just 30 men who fear nothing but God and hate nothing but sin and we will change the world.'

Isn't that what we want to be, world changers? Don't we want the Lord with us? Don't we want his awesome power to be carried around in our frail human bodies so that everybody we meet knows about it? Aren't we hungry for not only his presence but also his prosperity? Of course, I'm not talking about having vast wads of cash in our bank accounts, but having something far more exciting – God-given success in whatever we undertake.

Imagine the scenario if it could be said of us that WHATEVER we do the Almighty Creator God, who created the universe with a word, puts his resources at our disposal. Sounds good, doesn't it? Sounds like what we need if we are going to get the job done in the nation. We need to become the kind of people who truly know what it means to carry the Lord's presence and the Lord's prosperity. I believe that the life of King Hezekiah, especially as revealed in those few verses in 2 Kings 18, gives us some amazing keys to unlock a life of faithfulness to and fruitfulness for God that so few of us ever experience.

I think that's why you picked this book up. You want more too. You want your life to count. Yes? Good. So let's get on with it. But first, please just spend a few minutes of your time reading the two amazing accounts of Hezekiah's life: 2 Kings 18–20; 2 Chronicles 29–32.

1

A SMILE FOR
ALL OF US

When I was 17, a man called Val Grieve took me under his wing. Val was one of the best preachers I've known. He was also the worst and loudest singer I have ever come across. There was one more truly remarkable thing about him: he had a massive and infectious heart for God. Lots of the radical stuff that The Message tries to do by reaching young people in a relevant way was being done by Val years before we even started. In the sixties, he set up the Catacombs coffee bar in the centre of Manchester, reaching what they called the beat generation with the astoundingly good news of the gospel. He also had his fingers in plenty of other pies, like being chairman of the Manchester City Mission, a group which has been working on Manchester's toughest estates for the last 100 years or so.

Val died suddenly in 1998. He'd been preaching one Saturday down in London and then twice on the Sunday morning at our local church. He went home, had a massive heart attack and, BOOM! he was with the Lord. He left me loads of his sermon notes and several books, one of which I have probably used more than any other recently in my speaking preparation. The book goes by the funky title of *Sermon Outlines – Exegetical and Expository*, by W. H. Griffith. I'm not quite sure that I properly know the difference between exegetical and expository, but I do know that this little book of sermons from a guy who died in 1924, which cost Val the princely sum of £1, has changed my life. And right at the top of the pile of all the book's gems there's the sermon

W. H. Griffith preached some time at the start of the twentieth century on 2 Kings 18:5–7:

> Hezekiah trusted in the Lord, the God of Israel. There was no-one like him among all the kings of Judah, either before him or after him. He held fast to the Lord and did not cease to follow him; he kept the commands the Lord had given Moses. And the Lord was with him; he was successful in whatever he undertook.

Hezekiah's success came from God. He knew the Lord's approval and felt the warmth of his smile. Is it really possible that our lives can know that same smile of God that Hezekiah experienced? I really believe it can happen. But there's an 'if' flying about – a really big if. It will only happen if we are prepared to practise the disciplines and display the passions of a real man or woman of God. It's obvious not just from this verse but from the whole of the man's story: Hezekiah was a real, gutsy man of God. He wasn't perfect by any means, occasionally doing some really stupid things, but you've got to admit that the line saying that 'there was no-one like him among all the kings of Judah' was a serious pat on the back. Even King David, the original man after God's own heart, couldn't hold a candle to Hezekiah when it came to showing true godly commitment. Hezekiah was a guy sold out to God, so determined to have more than a 'nice' relationship with some distant deity that he aimed high and dreamed big. I think God quite likes that kind of attitude.

But do you want to know something really amazing? Take a look at Hezekiah's background. His family life could hardly be described as stable: Ahaz became Hezekiah's dad when he was aged just 13, and 7 short years later Ahaz was on the throne, totally ill-equipped to be either a king or a dad. He went on to become the original psycho-king, an extremely violent and deeply disturbed man who sank so deep into worship of Baal that he sacrificed several of Hezekiah's brothers in the fire (2 Kings 16:3; 2 Chronicles 28:3). As well as child sacrifice, Ahaz saw worship as a decent opportunity to encouraged homosexuality, temple prostitution and depraved orgies of witchcraft and violence.

So, Hezekiah probably had some issues to work through. Of course, it would have been easy for him to feel sorry for himself, to go along with the flow and keep up the family traditions. But something caught the fire of Hezekiah's imagination, making him determined not to let the pain of his past determine his destiny for the future.

What I've learned over the years is that God loves to use damaged goods just like Hezekiah. They end up getting taken on in a big way to work out his amazing plans. It often seems that those who have had tough and hurtful family experiences get a double dose. Just take a look at the great leaders of our day. Many of the ones who seem so together on the stage and are really cutting it in terms of making a difference for Jesus are actually from family backgrounds that are far from ideal. Lots of you will have heard Joyce Meyer share her childhood experiences of abuse and neglect, experiences which left her feeling damaged, rejected and lonely. Look at her now and you can see that there's a real authority surrounding her work and ministry. It's about more than the profile she has from being a TV evangelist, more than the cash she's been able to raise. Joyce Meyer's journeys through the pits of human experience have meant that she does more than just teach about suffering; she really understands and empathises with people's pain.

I am biased because they are my mates, but as far as I am concerned Mike Pilavachi and Matt Redman have been two of the most influential Christian leaders of the last generation. They've led tens of thousands of young people into a life of worship that involves more than just singing all those amazing Soul Survivor worship songs, but also putting it all into action among the lost and the poor.

What most don't know is that Mike's and Matt's ministries have a history marked by serious pain and hurt. Matt's dad died when he was a little boy, and the stepfather who moved into his family home didn't treat him very well. Mike's family moved over from Greece to the UK, when he was a little boy; he grew up unable to speak the language and unable to make friends. He was desperately lonely, and for several of his teenage years shut down completely. He went in on himself and only spoke the absolute essentials that were needed to get by. Both of them were damaged, both of them were pretty unlikely looking leaders, yet God's smile saw them grow into a pair of holy revolutionaries.

It was in the late 1980s – a few years before Mike and Matt started the Soul Survivor church plant with about a dozen of their friends – when they had the wacky idea of giving the best night of the week to God. For several months, just Mike and Matt would meet together, Matt strumming his guitar and the two of them singing worship songs, praying and praising the Lord all night long. It's at this point that you have to feel sorry for Matt: Mike is not a much better singer than Val Grieve. Still, I think God liked it. I think that the Lord saw something in these two young men as they spent their Saturday evenings worshipping, and I think that he felt free to bless them. Ever since, he has chosen to make them successful in so many of the things they've undertaken: Matt's songs are now sung all over the world, and Soul Survivor blesses hundreds of thousands of young people every year through their fast-growing church conferences, missions and worship resources.

About five years ago, Mike came to see me, and he was in a bit of a flap. Matt was feeling like it was time for him to move on from Soul Survivor, and Mike was wondering how Soul Survivor would manage without its key worship leader. I wasn't feeling at my most sensitive that day, and I suggested that if Soul Survivor stood or fell depending on Matt Redman's involvement, it was in deep trouble. Of course, what has happened is that God's smile is on the life of Mike Pilavachi and Soul Survivor, so much so that there was a young man who had also been in Mike's youth camp and was just coming out of university, namely Tim Hughes. He has filled Matt's big shoes and has written some of the most popular worship songs in the world. I like it when God makes lovely people like Mike successful in whatever they undertake.

What Mike and Matt have locked into is the simple fact that real godly success is primarily a matter of the heart. It's not about talent, sexiness, or even gifting. Hezekiah was not successful because of his position – there were plenty of kings (including his loopy dad) who were far from successful, messing up big time the lives of millions of people. But Hezekiah was more than just a man with influence and power: he had a good heart that longed to see God at the centre of the nation's life; he chose to be different.

All across the UK today, there are people getting up in the face of the gloom merchants, showing that there *are* wonderful things going on among young people and the church. It is true that we have lost a lot of young people from the churches over the last couple of decades but I've got a sense that most of those who are there now really want to be there and are in it for the long haul. Church decline is still scary and severe in lots of places but the young people I meet give me massive hope for the future. I think it's interesting that at the height of the Wesleyan revival, when thousands were becoming Christians and incredible manifestations of God's power were happening right across the nation, church decline was still at its steepest. However, the people who were saved through Wesley's work were so radical that they went out and multiplied. A generation later, the church reached its high-water mark and all that wonderful social reform took place.

When I look at the scene among young people in the UK, I see plenty of quality lives putting a radical faith into radical action. There are the ones who are serving long term – and often at great personal cost – on our inner-city Eden projects. There are others who pray round the clock as part of 24/7 Prayer, the largest youth prayer movement in history. There are the tens of thousands who, over the last few years, have paid out good money to get their hands dirty and serve on massive urban missions like Festival: Manchester and Soul in the City. These projects are springing up all over the place, and they leave me feeling full of hope for the future of the church in the UK.

I believe that when Jesus said: 'I will build my church, and the gates of Hades will not overcome it' (Matthew16:18) he really meant it. It's not just for Africa, South America or China, but for Europe too – the one continent in the world where the church of Jesus isn't growing at the moment. I believe that even the hellish forces of materialism, sexual promiscuity and pleasure for the sake of pleasure will not be able to stop Jesus building his church in his way.

I have the privilege of travelling around quite a bit and spending time with some brilliant youth ministries around the UK. One of my favourites is NGM, led by the irrepressible Ray and Nancy Goudie. Recently, I visited them in Bristol to encourage their team. Once again, I was blown away by the passion and fire of the young people who were out there doing the business: planting churches and presenting the good news in amazingly imaginative ways.

At the end of my talk, Ray invited the guys to pray for me. I was getting on with the job of being blessed until one of their young leaders, a man named Danny Budd, started praying for me. He quoted 2 Chronicles 16:9, a verse which says pretty much the same thing as our 2 Kings passage: 'For the eyes of the Lord range throughout the earth to strengthen those whose hearts are fully committed to him.' I was hugely challenged. Could it be that as the eyes of the Lord range the earth (which they do continually) when they rest on me they will find a heart fully after him? If he does find that kind of a heart, one that's totally fired up about being committed, then he will respond with a promise to strengthen us in all we do. How much I wanted that for our work in Manchester.

So what do you think? Before we even look at King Hezekiah and all he was able to achieve with God's blessing in place, how about we get real with where we're going with God? Do we want it to be said of us that we chased after him? Do we want to be part of God's plan to influence our church, our families, our communities and our friends? How about us being those men or women who are fully committed to him in our thought life, our finances, our attitudes and desires, our devotions and our service? How about being the kind of people who reserve their very best for God? One thing's for sure: if we are prepared to be those deliberately different people then our friends, classmates, colleagues and families will be line for some of God's blessing too.

Over the last few years, a little book by Bruce Wilkinson called *The Prayer of Jabez* has become an absolute phenomenon. The last I heard, it had sold around 15 million copies and had taken up residence at the top of the *New York Times* bestseller list. It's good stuff too, with some great teaching in it. But millions of Christians have now taken to praying the prayer of Jabez every day, as if it were some sort of spiritual mantra. Maybe they think that if they skip their prayer of Jabez for a day they'll miss out on their portion of blessing, that their territory won't be enlarged and that the Lord's hand won't be there to keep them from evil (1 Chronicles 4:10).

I have absolutely no problem with us asking God to bless us, as long as that's not all we pray for. The truth is that we are often guilty of not asking for enough from God. However, what most of us who pray the prayer of Jabez seem to forget is that immediately before the prayer appears in the Bible we read that 'Jabez was more honourable than his brothers.' In other words, there was no one like him. The people today who are on the receiving end of extraordinary blessing are, like Jabez, living extraordinary lives, not just praying funky little prayers. I've got a feeling that we get as blessed as we really want to be. The Lord's not fussy: he'll bless anyone! When he sees a heart fully inspired to follow him, when he finds someone outstandingly 'honourable', something simple yet wonderful happens: God pours out his blessings.

It's time to stop comparing ourselves with others. We look at them and claim that they are less spiritual than us, criticising their justifications and actions. We compare ourselves financially, criticising the richer ones for spending out on *that* home, *that* car or *that* iPod. Well, how about choosing some better comparisons? For example, how do we measure up against Jesus, the man who told us to 'be perfect' (Matthew 5:48) and who made it clear that 'as the Father has sent me, I am sending you' (John 20:21)? How about we compare ourselves with the vast majority of the world who are worse off financially and spiritually? How about we decide to do something about it?

We're not daft; we all want the smile of God on our lives, but how many of us are prepared to rise above the ordinary? How many are up for making Hezekiah's words our own and saying: 'I'm determined that there will be no one like me as I trust the Lord, hold fast to the Lord, follow the Lord and obey the Lord in my situation'?

It might not even need as many as Wesley's 30 men or women living radically to make something extraordinary happen in our situation. The great American evangelist Dwight L. Moody, who led thousands to the Lord at the end of the nine-teenth century, famously said: 'The world has yet to see what God can do with one man fully consecrated to him. By God's help I aim to be that man.' Interestingly, Moody was another one who had anything but an easy childhood. His father died suddenly in 1841, shortly after the family were hit by a disastrous financial crisis. He grew up in a family that experienced poverty, hard work and self-denial. His education was virtually non-existent, and it was said that when he first left his home town of Northfield, Massachusetts, at the age of 17, he could hardly string a sentence together. Yet this unlikely candidate had some of that Hezekiah DNA in his heart. He kept humble and went on to become the greatest evangelist and, according to many, the greatest man of his generation.

So how about it? Could we be that kind of man or woman? Could it be possible that we might have a remarkable future ahead of us? Surely the answer is yes. We've got to join in the shout with Mike, Matt, Joyce, Danny, John, Jabez, Dwight and millions more believers who have known that same smile of God. Just like Hezekiah, there is a simple answer to the question of our future: with God's help, we can!

2

A SMILE WORTH WAITING FOR

God's timing is a funny old thing. I may have been 17 when I recommitted my life to Jesus and believed that he had gifted me as an evangelist, but I had to wait another 15 years to go into full-time ministry. I pushed loads of doors along the way, tried to get things started a little earlier, but it seemed that for some reason God wanted me in the fashion industry even though I wanted to be out there on the front line of mission. I had a 400-year-old cottage and several lovely motors, but I knew I would never be really satisfied until I was giving all my time and energy to winning young people for Jesus.

I still don't know why I had to wait until I was 32 before I got to be a (slightly old) youth leader. I definitely felt too ageing to be in a funky rap outfit, but, as usual, God knew best. The last few years have been filled with more good things than I could have ever imagined when I was trucking up and down the motorway trying to sell our slightly tacky fashion accessories to the masses on the British high street. Perhaps what's important is being faithful where you are, as well as always being open for God to redirect you at any point.

Things started to speed up for Hezekiah in 726 BC, when he was 25 years old. It was shortly before his father's death, and things weren't going too well for his old man. It seems that the people were unhappy with King Ahaz, and his reign was brought to an early end. In 2 Chronicles 28:27 there is a particularly telling verse that lets us know that when he did die, Ahaz was 'not placed in the tombs of the kings of Israel'. That's a major snub for a king of Israel, but the man had made choices that had prompted inevitable consequences. In other words, because of his sinfulness and rebellion, Ahaz threw away what was his birthright as a king of Israel. I wonder, for how many people could something tragically similar be said at the end of their lives, that they missed out on so much of the blessing that God had planned for them? Ahaz learned 3,000 years ago that you can't make a fool of God, that one day we really will reap what we sow. Sow to please the sinful nature and you reap destruction; sow to please the Spirit and you reap eternal life (see Galatians 6:8). For Ahaz, after just about the worst reign Israel had ever experienced, it was disgrace and rejection all the way.

As Hezekiah made it to the throne and took on the responsibility of leading a nation in turmoil, he must have been completely daunted, fully aware of the extent to which he needed God's help. All Hezekiah could think to do was to get on with the job in hand and work flat out to get the people of Israel back on track with their God.

He knew that God's glory was at stake, and that a nation was missing out on the joy of a relationship with God, so he simply had to act without delay.

How much do we need that spirit in young men and women today? How vital is it that there are those around who have fallen in love with God and just can't bear the fact that he is not getting the praise he deserves in the nation? God is doing some wonderful things with worship but we need to realise that until we have a passion for seeing God worshipped by the rest of the world, we haven't really worshipped him in the first place. In other words, all real worship leads to mission. Once we have been in his presence, it shouldn't take us long before we are praying, planning and dreaming dreams to make him known to others.

That was what was going on in Hezekiah's heart as he went for it, unveiling his master plan. He got the people behind his vision to reopen the Temple, reinstate the priests and start worshipping, serving and giving to the Lord like never before. His first speech to the Levites in 2 Chronicles 29:5–11 burns with the fire of God and the desire to see him praised. 'Our fathers were unfaithful ...', he rants, explaining why they are living under God's judgement. 'I intend to make a covenant with the Lord ... so that his fierce anger will turn away from us. My sons, do not be negligent now, for the Lord has chosen you ...'

That must have been some serious sweet-sounding music in the ears of Father God as this young guy challenged the people to turn back to him. I believe the Lord is on the lookout for similar young people who will challenge others at this low point in our spiritual history to 'not be negligent now, for the Lord has chosen you ...'

What could be more negligent than going with the flow of this 'me! Me! ME!' generation? All around us is the pressure to focus our thoughts, desires and plans on how we can acquire more and more things, the kind of things that we know deep down inside will never truly satisfy. At the same time, the name of the Lord is dishonoured. For many people, it's as if the temple door to the

Lord is firmly nailed shut, leaving them with the feeling that God has no place in their lives. And so, just as with Hezekiah, it is our job to go and bear fruit for God. I believe that in an even greater way than for Hezekiah – who, despite being a king of Israel, couldn't experience the constant fullness of the Spirit in the way we can in this New Testament age – we have a future worth getting excited about. When we became Christians, God already knew the good things he had planned in advance for us to do (Ephesians 2:10). For eternity, God has been dreaming up unique ways that we can be used by him. He's been working on what Andy Hawthorne Fruit might look like, making it unique to me. Of course, you've got yours too, and the fun of being a Christian is waking up every day and being able to say: 'OK God, you promised in the Bible that you've chosen and appointed me to bear plenty of long-life fruit. So today I'm going to do it!'

An even more exciting thought is that every time we are fruitful for God, pointing others to him and fighting for his glory, the good stuff starts to multiply. Every prayer, every bit of generosity, every kind action, every sensitive word spoken has a ripple effect that spreads further than we might imagine. The fact is that we never just influence one person for God; that person sits at the centre of ever-expanding spheres of contact. As they get to know Jesus, their school, college, workplace, family and street are never quite the same. You never know how much things will multiply, or where it will all end up, but ever since the dawn of time God's blessings have sent shock waves across the planet.

Heaven's got to be good. But of all the unspeakably wonderful things God has saved for us there, one of the best things is going to be seeing all the people who have played a part in us being there. I think that quite a few million years might well be taken up with people saying thank you for the gifts people made of vision, prayers, money, words and energy. All these connections that feed into our own lives may take quite some untangling, but I think it'll be worth it. So much of the stuff we do on earth may be a laugh but it's gone in a moment. The God stuff we do really does last for ever. Seeing that take its place in eternity is going to be the biggest buzz of them all.

I'm sure Hezekiah didn't know what was about to happen when he reopened the Temple and reinstated the priests. He just knew it was the right thing to do, and as God saw Hezekiah's heart he decided to bless his efforts. The result? A massive revival broke out across the nation. Matt Redman has described ministry as being like surfing: it often takes a long time to get up, and often you keep falling over. But once you do get up and there's a wave behind you, you can go a very long way in a very short space of time.

I don't want it to sound as if I am comparing the work of a funny Manchester rap outfit to one of Israel's greatest ever kings, but I must confess that in the early days of the World Wide Message Tribe we definitely felt like we knew a little of what Hezekiah was going through. We were locked into God's purposes, and things were happening quickly. It had all come out of the sheer frustration from seeing what looked like a whole generation of kids growing up in inner-city Manchester, for whom Jesus was little more than a swear word. Despite the fact that there were lots of lively churches in the suburbs, these people were pretty much pagan.

OK, so we weren't kings; we didn't have loads of money or contacts, and in fact I couldn't even sing, dance or rap very well. But we did have a heart to tell these young people about Jesus. As a result, God definitely did things quicker than we could have ever imagined. We'd planned to go from school to school a week at a time, using the music as a platform for the good news. Before we knew it, we were seeing loads of young people becoming Christians, selling hundreds of thousands of albums, winning awards, filling the biggest venues in the city and dreaming up a strategy to see the whole of Manchester soaked with the love of Jesus. When God gets hold of things, they definitely happen fast.

Recently, I was at Soul Survivor, hanging around at the end of a seminar. A stream of young people came to see me, each with stories of how they had either been impacted by or become Christians through the band. They all wanted to tell me the fantastic things they were doing for God, working on estates or training for ministry or involved in youth work. I realised again that God had smiled and multiplication had kicked in.

Revival: the ripple effect

It's worth us taking a bit of a look at 2 Chronicles 29. It's there that we get to see the full-on revival that broke out on the back of Hezekiah's faithfulness. It's clear from this passage that revival doesn't just fill the pews, but it also transforms communities.

Before we start, it's worth pointing out that we never quite know the exact date of revival. It can't be predicted, as the timing and action is all down to God. Not long ago, I spoke about revival at a Christian conference. I gave the seminar the title 'Keys to Revival'. It wasn't until I was halfway through my preparation that I realised what a poor title that was. There is only one key that will unlock true revival, and God's got that one. However, there are definite signs that God is up to something, and there are important priorities that believers need to have if they want to help get the ground ready for God's actions.

It's all nicely clear in 2 Chronicles 29. As well as the obvious point that our prayers need to be united, there are a few other things we need to keep in mind if we really do want to see a major move of God:

A new holiness

The first thing that the Bible says about Hezekiah in verse 2 is that he 'did what was right in the eyes of the Lord'. Later on, we'll look at the characteristics of Hezekiah from 2 Kings 18, characteristics that made him a man who enjoyed the Lord's presence and prosperity, but for now let's just leave it that he was a godly man. When God is about to do something big, a new hatred of sin gets into the veins of his church. We find we just can't do the stuff we used to do. Other Christians may be able to justify living against God's commands, but because we long to be a revival people we have to clean up our act. Hezekiah's charge to the priests was not just to consecrate the Temple (v. 5) but also to consecrate themselves. This wasn't so that they could have a nice time of praise but so that the Lord's 'fierce anger' would 'turn away from' them (v. 10). If we long for real revival to sweep away so much of the dross that we live with in this nation, we have got to spend time reflecting on our behaviour and attitudes. We simply have to turn our backs on anything that isn't right in the eyes of the Lord, choosing instead to head for the things are right. You can rest assured that God wants you to be holy more than you do. If you ask him to show you the stuff that's wrong, it won't take long before you find out.

A new urgency

Revival people are always passionate, driven people. They are the sort who simply don't hang around being bored but instead get on with making a difference. Hezekiah didn't take time out to settle gently into his role, finding out how the system worked and who did what in the palace: 'On the first month of the first year of his reign' (v. 3) he reopened the Temple, reinstated the priests and called the people to worship. He couldn't stand it for one day longer that God wasn't getting the glory he deserved, so at his first opportunity he did all he could. I imagine Hezekiah in his late teens and early twenties dreaming about what he would do when his moment came. He had a plan and vision for his life that involved milking it for God's praise.

Recently, I met Reinhard Bonnke. He's one of the most passionate, driven people anywhere. He told me that a few years ago he was an unknown missionary in Burkina Faso, travelling from village to village in his VW van preaching to a few dozen people at a time. But God saw his heart. For three nights running, he had a dream of Africa being washed in the blood of Jesus. At the same time, he heard the voice of the Lord saying: 'Africa will be saved.' He asked his wife what he should do. She wasn't sure, but figured that whatever he did it ought to be pretty quick. And so, driven by a new urgency, he booked the local football stadium for a mission. You can guess what came next: multiplication kicked in. Now he has literally millions turning up at his mission all over Africa, and experiences the most extraordinary salvation and miracles.

In his book *Evangelism by Fire*, he writes about the urgency for the gospel that we are supposed to have:

The Gospel is eternal, but we haven't eternity to preach it. One would think we had that long when we view the often leisurely operations of the Church on the Gospel front. We have only as long as we live to reach those who live as long as we live. Today, over five billion souls are alive – alive in our present world, not in an indefinite future age which needs to be evangelised. *It is the last hour.*[1]

---

[1] *Evangelism by Fire* by Reinhard Bonnke (Kingsway, 1994), p. 23.

A new expectancy

God just loves faith. He loved the fact that Hezekiah was prepared to stand up in front of so many people and say: 'I intend to make a covenant with the Lord ...' (v. 10). In other words, he was telling them that they could keep on with their lousy Baal religion; nothing was going to stop him praising God. God loved it that this young guy had the expectancy to go to the city officials (v. 20) and tell them of his plan. At any point, the priests, the city officials, or the rest of the elite could have told him to get lost, but there was a vision raging in his heart. He had the faith to believe that God would bless the vision that drove him on. How we need young men and women with expectant faith and vision who truly believe that if they step out of their comfort zone and do the right thing then God will do the rest. It's a sure sign of revival when people like that start to spring up all over the place.

New praise

It seems that right at the heart of every real revival there has been a new sense of adoration. So often it seems that awesome new songs of praise help to capture the hearts of believers, a bit like in verses 25–30:

> He stationed the Levites in the temple of the Lord with cymbals, harps and lyres in the way prescribed by David and Gad the king's seer and Nathan the prophet; this was commanded by the Lord through his prophets. So the Levites stood ready with David's instruments, and the priests with their trumpets.
>
> Hezekiah gave the order to sacrifice the burnt offering on the altar. As the offering began, singing to the Lord began also, accompanied by trumpets and the instruments of David king of Israel. The whole assembly bowed in worship, while the singers sang and trumpeters played. All this continued until the sacrifice of the burnt offering was completed.
>
> When the offerings were finished, the king and everyone present with him knelt down and

worshipped. King Hezekiah and his officials ordered the Levites to praise the Lord with the words of David and of Asaph the seer. So they sang praises with gladness and bowed their heads and worshipped.

Wouldn't you love to have been there? Spring Harvest and Soul Survivor couldn't even come close. Back then, the cymbals, harps and lyres (v. 25) were on the cutting edge of musical innovation. David was the king who had taken the bold step of bringing them into the worship setting, so it's a little like saying: 'Praise him with the sample machine, the fat beats, the DJ's decks.' Whatever you've got – give glory to God with it.

The songs that have formed the soundtrack to recent revivals have placed Jesus firmly at the heart of things. I love reading about the times during the Welsh, Hebridean and Wesleyan revivals when the meetings got hijacked by the glory of God. People were so caught up in it all that the meetings just couldn't be finished. At some points, they had to close the meetings at breakfast time in order for the people to go to work. Only once or twice have I tasted a little of what that is like, and it really is the best thing in the world.

New songs, new praise and a new sense of God's presence always seem to be a sign that God is up to something.

New sacrifice

On the back of this awesome time of praise, Hezekiah invited the people 'whose hearts were willing' (v. 31) to join him and make their praises known to God. The method chosen was the thank-offering, an opportunity for people to bring what they wanted to the Temple as a sign of their appreciation of God's blessings. Hezekiah was overwhelmed by the response as the people – many of whom were poor and out of work under the old Ahaz regime – brought almost 4,000 bulls, lambs and goats for sacrifice. In fact, there were so many offerings that the priests simply couldn't keep up with skinning the things (v. 34). 'There were burnt offerings in abundance, together with the fat of the fellowship offerings and the drink offerings that accompanied the burnt offerings' (v. 35). The people had locked into the fact that because God was so great they were compelled to give him thanks. He'd forgiven them loads, and they couldn't help but be generous in return. I'm convinced that as the smell of those sacrifices wafted up to heaven they were a pretty sweet odour in the nostrils of God. He knew that it meant his people were leaving behind the mess they'd made of things. They were coming back.

Today, God's not looking for burnt offerings. He's far more interested in 'living sacrifices' (Romans 12:1) who choose not to live by the world's standards but to be transformed by getting their heads sorted out by God. And without those living sacrifices, we ain't going to see a revival. We can have all the new faith, new praise, new holiness and urgency that we like, but without the sacrifice that puts God first and us second, we simply aren't going to get what we want.

But what does being a living sacrifice mean? It

differs for each of us, and we must ask God to show us our own path. It might mean that we build our lives around being able to fund God's work instead of indulging in our every extravagance. It might mean that we go to live among the poor, or that we carve out sacrificial time to pray for the needs of the world. Whatever the plan, be sure that God, if we ask him, will let us know what our part is. One thing is for sure: it will definitely involve great sacrifice. As we'll discover later, we are called to follow Jesus, the man who sacrificed the lot for us. He couldn't have put it much more simply than this: 'Unless you forsake all you can't be my disciple' (which is the gist of Mark 8:34). I really want to be a disciple of Jesus, and I know that it's the only way to enjoy life fully here and go to heaven when I die. God is right now looking for people who are committed to laying their lives down for him. Yes, getting the smile of God costs. But like all good things, a little effort on our part makes the reward all the sweeter.

New acceleration

Put all this repentance, urgency, faith, high praise and sacrifice in the mix and add to it God's decision to revive us; then things start to happen quickly. I love the last verse of Chronicles 29: 'Hezekiah and all the people rejoiced at what God had brought about for his people, because it was done so quickly.'

All the revival stories in the Bible are littered with words like suddenly, speedily and quickly. My consistent experience has been that doing stuff for God seems to involve nothing, a little more nothing, followed by a whole chunk of more nothing. Then, just when you get so frustrated that you realise you can't do this thing on your own and you start to really pray, along comes a something. God speaks – as he always does when you give him time – and suddenly, speedily, quickly everything happens.

We live in a totally self-obsessed society that promises so much and delivers so little. Our mantra of 'minimal effort, instant gratification' goes against the route we have to travel to find God's smile. But make no mistake: God is on the lookout for those revival people who have taken the time to lay the vital foundations in their lives. Why? So that when he's ready he can quickly build the kind of revival that we so desperately need. Of course you're up for it.

3

A SMILE WORTH TRUSTING

*'Hezekiah trusted in the Lord,
the God of Israel'*

So if it takes time to build the essential foundations needed to get a full-on blazing smile
from the Lord, it kind of makes sense that there
will be times when we're left wondering whether
it really is worth all the waiting. So this is where
the issue of trust jumps its way to the front of the
queue. If we can't allow God to do his things in
his perfect timing, then we're going to find the
waiting pretty hard going.

We started The Message Trust in 1992 with just one employee and an annual turnover of around £20,000. Back then, it was a total faith adventure, and even though these days the turnover is about 100 times bigger, it's still a daily journey that we can only get through by choosing to trust God for every little thing. Each month, we need people and pounds to flesh out the vision that drives us on. Each month, we get an excellent opportunity to put our faith to the test.

As I'm writing, we are once again three days away from pay day for the 60 or so full-time staff at The Message Trust. As ever, we still need to see tens of thousands of pounds come in to meet all the bills. I wish it got easier after 13 years but it doesn't. I also happen to think – although only in my better moments – that I wouldn't have it any other way. Over the years, God has proved himself incredibly faithful, and we've learned so much through this slightly precarious faith lifestyle.

I often teach the students on our training programme 'Genetik' that if you aren't in a place where you are stuffed if God doesn't turn up for you, get there. Our God is determined that we learn to trust him entirely and will often take us through some pretty tricky experiences to get us there.

So now it's time to get down to the nitty-gritty and work out just what it was about Hezekiah that so drew the Lord's attention. What did the man do that meant God felt free to send the revival that shook the nation of Israel all those years ago? There's probably no scripture that sums it up quite as well as the touchstone verses in 2 Kings 18:5–7:

> Hezekiah trusted in the Lord, the God of Israel. There was no-one like him among all the kings of Judah, either before him or after him. He held fast to the Lord and did not cease to follow him; he kept the commands the Lord had given Moses. And the Lord was with him; he was successful in whatever he undertook.

Impressive? Yes. These four characteristics at the core of this man not only drew the smile of God towards his life and work, but sustained him in the build-up. And guess what: these are the exact four characteristics that we need to build into our lives if we also want to be used for high and holy purposes. Do you want to live a life that counts? This four-step plan makes it about as simple as it can possibly be, and we'll tuck into them in turn throughout the rest of the book.

Of course, the first one is faith. 'Hezekiah trusted in the Lord,' it says. Someone clever once said that faith is the most explosive thing in the universe. I'm not much of an authority on explosives, so I'll take their word for it. What I do know is that according to the Bible it's through faith that:

1. We are made right with God in the first place.
2. We are able to come right into his presence.
3. We receive his Spirit into our lives.
4. We have Jesus with us continually.

The Bible goes on to say that 'without faith it is impossible to please God' (Hebrews 11:6) and that everything is possible for him who has faith

(Mark 9:23). In other words, faith is vitally important, so it's no wonder that it happens to be the first quality listed of this man of God. We can have great vision and a good character but without the explosive spark of faith nothing is going to happen. How do we get it? It's an odd one, but faith is a gift that we get despite the fact that we simply don't deserve it. Like all the other great things that God hands out to us, we have to trust that what the Lord says is true and then have the bottle to turn his commands into action. If we want faith, we've got to live it.

I remember learning about a guy who had fallen out with his brother-in-law. He was upset about it and wanted to make it up to him. So he went out and bought him an extra-expensive Christmas present. However, instead of ripping off the paper, the brother-in-law just left it under the Christmas tree. On the twelfth night, when it was time to put the decorations away, he took the present and threw it into the garbage, still wrapped in its Christmas paper. It's a bleak story, but could this be a reasonably accurate picture of so many of our lives? God has so many good gifts he wants to pour into our lives but because we refuse to open them, because we don't have the faith to try them out, they sit unwrapped. Finally, at the end of our lives, they will be thrown out, never to be enjoyed by us or by the world around us.

That is exactly what King Ahaz did, and precisely what King Hezekiah didn't do. From the moment that Hezekiah had the opportunity to put his faith to the test, he got on with it. It seems that the whole story of God working out his master plan of salvation, even from the dawn of time, has been all about faith. And guess what: if we want to be part of what he's doing in this generation, we are going to need to be a people of faith.

It's great to read of the heroes of the faith in Hebrews 11, guys like: Abel, who was full of faith; Enoch who walked by faith; Noah, whose whole family was saved by faith, and Abraham, whose faith took him away from his home and made him willing even to sacrifice his son. There were people like Daniel, whose faith saved him from the lions, and Elijah, whose faith brought back the dead. But Hebrews 11 also celebrates guys like Jeremiah, who was beaten and imprisoned, Zechariah, who was stoned, and Hezekiah's contemporary, the great prophet Isaiah, who, we believe, was sawn in half. Living by faith is not always the easy option, but it is certainly the only option for those who are serious about doing the business for God.

Of course, the good news is that the faith story doesn't end with the Old Testament greats. The New Testament is the story of so-called 'unschooled' and ordinary men and women who were full of faith and the Holy Spirit and doing the most wacky things through them in Jesus' name. They started by filling Jerusalem with the teaching of Jesus (see Acts 5:28), and before they knew it they had turned the world upside down with their teaching (see Acts 17:6). There were guys like Philip who, acting by faith, obeyed the strange promptings of the Spirit and was inspired to lead the first Samaritan and the first African to Jesus (Acts 8:4–8, 26–40). Then there was

Ananias, who, despite all the evidence that he might get his head chopped off, took the love of Jesus to the man Christians feared most at the time, the arch-persecutor Saul (Acts 9:10–19). There was Peter, the one who left his religious baggage behind and was prepared to cross the great religious divide and take the gospel to the Gentiles (Acts 10). And of course, we shouldn't forget maybe the greatest man of faith ever, Paul, who exploded the gospel all over the known world. Together, this collection of individual stories is one continuous demonstration of faith in the risen Jesus, which is based on an essential truth: Jesus is God; he said he would build a mighty church and that he loves using ordinary people like us, so by faith we are going to get on with it.

These stories are a great inspiration, yet if we are not careful we can treat them a bit like the latest Christian paperback thrillers. We get excited, inspired and encouraged in all the right places but we fail to make the connection between what God did in their lives and what he can do in ours. Before we know it, the book is on the shelf and we're settling back into our mundane life that is so much less than God wants for us. Where's God's smile? The truth is that we don't stick around long enough with the risks to find out.

Every single man or woman of great faith became the way they are because they decided to make a change. They made up their minds to live differently, resolving to give God everything. We can call it 'walking by faith' if you like, or taking risks for God. Either way, God knew their good intentions and turned things to the good. What's really great is that faith is not a prize that we can win, an accomplishment that we can acquire, tick off and forget about. For each of these inspiring names, God made sure that the faith muscle got a decent workout. He continually offered them fresh challenges, all the time pushing them on to be able to achieve even more for him. You know, I think that it would be fantastic if some of you who read this book put it down and said, 'That's it! I'm tired of reading chapter 1 in the Old Testament or chapter 2 in the book of Acts: I'm going to write my own faith chapter!' And why not?

Why don't you get yourself lined up with some godly giving, serving and living where you're 100 per cent truly stuffed if God doesn't show up and help out?

Someone who did just that was Liza Fawcett. She's one of our Eden workers who has chosen to live long term on one of the toughest estates in Manchester. Why? Because she wants to be at the heart of an amazing faith-fuelled story, seeing the kingdom come in these spiritual wastelands. Liza, however, is far from an ordinary Eden worker (if there is such a thing). First of all, unlike most of the team, who are in their early to mid-twenties, she is seventy-four years old. Yet when she heard me speak about Eden for the first time, her heart jumped. It made sense that if Eden means simply living as salt and light, praying for and loving our neighbours, then it doesn't matter how old we are. She was right. So, after coming to visit Manchester and talking to her church leadership, she decided to sell her picturesque cottage. This wasn't any picturesque cottage, but one set in the middle of what is officially the poshest part of

Britain today. Out of over 34,000 wards, hers was recognised as being the most privileged in which to live, but Liza left and moved to the other end of the scale. In fact, she ended up in what is officially the worst ward in the whole country, Harpurhey, determined to help reach that community for Jesus.

Someone at the *Manchester Evening News* heard about this remarkable lady, and so the paper printed a full-page article about Liza's faith step. In the article, Liza said something really beautiful: 'The truth is, I have never been as fulfilled.' What had happened was that through her sacrifice and faith, Liza had locked into the law of the universe: you can't out-give God. She'd started to experience the kind of eternal success that has nothing to do with nice cottages and posh neighbours, but everything to do with serving Jesus and serving his world. And to do it took faith. She had to trust that God's smile would be there when she moved, even though it was just about the most upside-down decision anyone in a posh picturesque cottage would choose to make.

Before she moved to Manchester, Liza's church had been turned upside down by the ministry of John Wimber. As far as I'm concerned, John Wimber is another guy who had the smile of God all over his life. As such, his influence has gone into big-time multiplication mode, with his simple message about the importance of getting open to God spreading further than any would have predicted. It was through John Wimber's bold Bible teaching on signs and wonders and the power of the Spirit that Holy Trinity Brompton was, in a manner of speaking, set on fire. As a result, the Alpha Course came into being, with its associated ministries blessing the nation like nothing else over the last decade. Wimber's influence was also felt at Liza's church, St Andrew's, Chorleywood. It was transformed, and as a result the New Wine network and Soul Survivor were born. The more you think about it, the more we have to thank this cuddly Californian for.

Of all the things that Wimber was famous for saying, his thoughts about the nature of faith hit the mark for me. He reckoned that faith is spelt

R–I–S–K. and, of course, he is right: there has to be a risk element to all our steps of faith. We've got to jump into the light, leaving our comfort zones and risking everything on God. That's what every believer is meant to do.

So I was therefore a little surprised at first when I heard my friend Mike Breen preaching at New Wine and saying that he felt faith was spelt S–U–R–E. He was quoting the Bible's most famous verse on the subject, Hebrews 11:1, 'Now faith is being sure of what we hope for and certain of what we do not see.' I was left with my head spinning a bit, thinking, 'Is it R–I–S–K., or is it S–U–R–E.?' You'll be glad to know I've decided that they're both right. Faith is not some licence to do stupid risky things for the sake of them; it is built on God's sure and certain word, which he will back up with all the resources of heaven. In other words, once we have understood what God's S–U–R–E. word is, we can take all sorts of R–I–S–K.

Hezekiah knew it was God's sure and certain plan that the Temple was open for worshippers, that the sacrificial system he had initiated was reinstated and that the Levites he'd chosen for priestly duties were given their jobs back. It was all there in the Bible, revealed clearly by God. In fact, it was a no-brainer, so Hezekiah was able to take some major faith risks, safe in the knowledge that he could trust God to back things up. That's true. And I bet it felt pretty scary too: Hezekiah put it all on the line.

Sometimes we Christians go wrong in our faith by failing to spend the necessary time and effort listening to God and studying his word. Without these disciplines, it is impossible for us to know what his plan is for our lives, or just how he wants us to exert our faith in a particular situation.

After the great faith chapter, Hebrews 12 starts off like this: 'Therefore, since we are surrounded by such a great cloud of witnesses, let us throw off everything that hinders and the sin that so easily entangles, and let us run with perseverance the race marked out for us.' The truth is that God has a race marked out just for you. I'm sure you realise it's more of a marathon than a sprint, and that it's a race that's full of challenge – the sort that takes loads of perseverance. But it's also a race that is glorious, the sort that will involve all sorts of surprises and delights around every corner.

Spending time with God is a no-brainer too, the kind of thing that it's impossible to wipe off the menu. If you want your own race of faith to get an overhaul, to take on fresh supplies of passion, expectation and excitement, then the solution is simple: spend time with God and the Bible, trying to suss out what the path ahead of you will look like. You can hold on to the certain truth that the Lord is with you, just as he was with Hezekiah, as well as all the great cloud of witnesses in Hebrews 11 and all the heroes of the early church.

While it might be tempting to think that we're in for less of an exciting ride than other Christians, it is simply not true. There are not two Holy Spirits: a Premier League one, who filled the disciples and the greats of history, and then a kind of Northern Conference Holy Spirit left for all the rejects like us. No way! There is only one

Holy Spirit. There is one source of power and possibility. He inspired the heroes of old and he's there for us too, helping us run our faith-filled race right to the end, all the way to the biggest smile of them all.

4

A Smile Behind the Clouds

'He held fast to the Lord'

I'm afraid to say I often used to boast about money. As The Message increased year by year we always were able to pay our staff on time, and so telling people about God's provision seemed like a pretty good thing to do. Often, we only made the deadlines by the skin of our teeth. However, each month, as we would look at the ever-increasing amount of 'faith' money needed for the expanding vision and get on our knees, God always provided. It wasn't unusual for us to be waiting until the last week of the month before the money came in, and occasionally it would be the very last day that we'd open the post and jump around the office because God, through his people, had pulled it off once again.

On one particular occasion, I even had all the team leaders waiting for me in our meeting-room. They didn't know that I was about to tell them we couldn't pay the salaries and would have to look at cutting back if we didn't see a large amount of money coming in fast, when, on the way to the meeting the phone went. It was a business friend calling to tell me he was going to send us £100,000 (the largest ever donation we had had up to that point). He paid it direct into our bank the next day. The meeting had gone from a time of weeping and wailing to a time of dancing! In hindsight, it must have been quite annoying for other struggling ministries to hear my triumphalist rants about God's miraculous provision.

I write that I *used to* boast about money because in Easter 2004 the pattern changed. After twelve years of living with the sound theory that God will always provide, it felt like God had a change of plan. Not only did the money stop rolling in but it felt as though we were experiencing opposition on all fronts: there was an increase in violence on our inner-city Eden projects; one of our high-tech Eden buses was mysteriously set on fire in the middle of the night; the other bus was trashed by vandals; at The Message, there suddenly seemed to be lots of difficult personal issues to deal with. So we fasted, we prayed, we wept and we wailed, but for the first time ever, we simply could not pay the salary bill on time.

Something else happened. For the first time since we started the Trust, my confidence took a serious knock. I've never been short of ideas for advancing God's kingdom – admittedly not all of them are good ideas, which is why it's good to have a team to help you sift the wheat from the chaff – but this time I couldn't even get my head above water long enough to have a *bad* idea, let alone one worth getting vaguely excited about. It really did feel as though the heavens were made of brass. There were times during that spring of 2004 when I seriously questioned whether I could stand the hassle of it all much longer. Of course, we all get there sooner or later; we all go through times of real difficulty. The only surprise is that it took God twelve years to hand out our big lesson on just how important it is that we hold on to the smile of God, no matter how far removed it feels.

Even though I was pretty stuck for ideas at the time, God was giving us loads of messages about us being on the verge of a time of unprecedented growth and financial provision. This was annoying.

We've always taken a day each month to pause whatever work we're doing and get together to pray and worship, always inviting a speaker to come and stir us up from the Bible and encourage us to keep going. In April, it was Judith Butler's turn. She came with a sense that we were on the verge of something big and that we were about to move from a place of 'just enough' to a place of 'more than enough'. I didn't have the heart to tell her that we were actually stuck in a place of 'nowhere near enough' at the time. The following month, it was the wonderful David Shearman, who reminded us of the Israelites moving from manna to a land flowing with milk and honey. He said that this was exactly what was about to happen for the ministry.

Things continued to get worse for the Trust over the next month, so when it was time for our June visitors to arrive, I was feeling slightly less than positive about the whole thing. It was the turn of our good friends, Gordon and Rachel Hickson, and I introduced them by announcing that if they prophesied that we were about to move into a time of great financial blessing I might just have to chin them. Rachel looked worried and whispered in Gordon's ear. She stood up and explained how God had woken her up at 3 am the previous morning and given her the strongest sense that great financial provision was coming our way, and that we were about to move from a time of just enough to a time of more than enough. She gave me two fifty-pound notes and said: 'This is a seed; you just watch what God does in the future.' I didn't know whether to laugh or cry, but I decided that it was about time I got the message.

One thing's for sure: it was still a while before we saw any sort of a turnaround. It even got worse, as the next month, for the first time ever, we had to lay off staff and cancel events – events at which I knew young people would get saved. Our financial director said that we needed £100,000 fast or we really would be in trouble. I got in a bit of a state about it all: was it something we were doing wrong (was there sin in the camp?), or was it something we were doing right (was it a test of faith?). The truth, I believe, was a bit of both. God will sometimes hold back the good stuff in our lives to grab our attention and get us to sort out things that aren't quite right. Maybe we had become a bit arrogant and presumptuous. Maybe we did need to examine our lives and make sure we were still on track. But I'm also sure that God wanted us to learn a massive lesson: that he can be trusted, even when it feels like everything is going against us. Tough as it may be, we will grow up to be bigger, better believers if we will just stick with him, even if sometimes it feels like we are just about hanging on by our fingernails.

Perhaps the most helpful thing that anyone said during the whole difficult period came from Mike Breen. He sent me an email, explaining that he thought we were experiencing what he called 'the supernatural/natural process of pruning for growth mentioned in John 15'. I think he was right. Isn't it great to have the Bible to illuminate things when stuff isn't going quite the way you want it to? Over the next few weeks, I devoured John 15:1–2, where Jesus says:

> I am the true vine, and my Father is the gardener. He cuts off every branch in me that bears no fruit, while every branch that does bear fruit he prunes so that it will be even more fruitful.

I knew for sure that we weren't an unfruitful branch at The Message, so what must have been going on was the painful process of pruning for greater growth. Sooner or later, it's going to happen to every one of us because Jesus, the master gardener, is determined that we produce maximum fruit for him during our short life here on earth; there will be times when he has to cut us back so that we can do just that. It's like the tree outside our kitchen window. It's an extra large, beautiful bright yellow acacia tree that is bursting with life. Twelve months ago I thought my wife Michele had killed it as she pruned it back to the very first signs of growth. The poor tree sat there looking like a slightly embarrassed naked stump. But of course it wasn't long before the result of the pruning was clear to see: the tree exploded with growth.

Around the middle of July, just after Collette had told us we needed £100,000, things changed. It was as if the lesson had been learned and, for some reason known only to God, he unscrewed the taps and allowed people to give again. The money started to flow, and within four weeks we were back on our feet. As well as the cash, it was as if God was speaking louder and clearer than ever, and over that summer period we found ourselves heading in new directions with the work of the Trust. We started dreaming dreams of training and releasing others through Genetik, and have moved towards evangelising whole regions at a time. I'm convinced this will be our most fruitful period so far.

The Bible offers so many wonderful promises for believers, but one thing it never promises is an easy ride. Face facts: it is going to be harder being a Christian than not being a Christian. Getting to hell is a piece of cake, especially if you're planning on living an unfruitful life in the process. There's absolutely no pruning required, and all you have to do is precisely, um, nothing. But for those of us who choose heaven, who want to be fruitful and see our gifts get seriously multiplied, we can be sure that ahead of us is more than our fair share of pruning, refining and hellish opposition.

Even in the life of Mr 'Presence and Prosperity' Hezekiah, we can see lots of opposition as well as lots of mistakes being made along the way. Straight after the amazing 'Revival Jerusalem' in 2 Chronicles 29, Hezekiah received an even bigger

dream: revival across the whole of Israel. This is
the way that things seem to happen with people
who listen to God: there's always another plan to
get excited about. And so, full of faith, 2 Chronicles 30 explains how the king sends out his
couriers with an invitation for the whole nation
to come and join in the wonderful worship in
Jerusalem. It was time to get back to basics and
celebrate the Passover to the Lord, the God of
Israel. What with things having gone so well
down there in Jerusalem, I'm sure that Hezekiah
must have been confident. He must have fully
expected the people to receive the envoys with
joy, to repent and then hot foot their way to the
Passover. The last thing he expected was for the
couriers to be met with scorn and ridicule (2
Chronicles 30:10). Yet Hezekiah was a man who,
according to the Bible, stuck things out with
God, even when he seemed far off. The king was
literally glued to the Lord, and no amount of discouragement was ever going to pull them apart.
So, as always with God, he had a divine 'but' up
his sleeve:

Nevertheless, some men of Asher, Manasseh and Zebulun humbled themselves and went to Jerusalem. Also in Judah the hand of God was on the people to give them unity of mind to carry out what the king and his officials had ordered, following the word of the Lord. (2 Chronicles 30:11–12)

Despite the discouragement and pruning that come our way, God is still doing his thing, still in charge, and his plans will not be sabotaged. For Hezekiah, it meant that actually he had fewer people at Passover than he had dreamed of. Many of the people stayed at home sneering and criticising but those who came were enough, enough to hold an incredible Passover feast with great worship and a willing sacrifice. In fact, it was so good that the people who were there begged for it to be extended for a further seven days. Not bad, huh? It was also good enough to inspire them to do the even more significant thing of smashing the Asherah poles and sacred stones and destroying the high places and altars of the Baal religion that had the nation seriously messed up (2 Chronicles 31:1).

By the end of chapter 31, Hezekiah is really on a roll. He has shown the people how to tuck into the act of sacrificial giving by providing thousands of bulls and sheep and goats for the seven days of the extended celebration (2 Chronicles 30:23–24). After that, he gave generously to the Levites for the morning and evening offerings. As always happens to those leaders who have the faith and are prepared to make the sacrifice, the others catch on too. This time, he ordered the people in Jerusalem to follow his lead and give the priests and Levites what they needed so that they could devote themselves to the Lord (2 Chronicles 31:4).

This time around, there wasn't quite so much sneering and criticising:

They brought a great amount, a tithe of everything. The men of Israel and Judah who lived in the towns of Judah also brought a tithe of their herds and flocks and a tithe of the holy things dedicated to the Lord their God, and they piled them in heaps. They began doing this in the third month and finished in the seventh month. When Hezekiah and his officials came and saw the heaps, they praised the Lord and blessed his people Israel. (2 Chronicles 31:5–8)

Hezekiah had been faithful; he had stuck things out and believed in God. He had refused to back down at the first sign of discouragement, and the results were astounding: God blessed him in the most extraordinary way, so much so that soon the revival vibe had spread right across the land of Judah. At the end of chapter 31, we are left with these amazing words:

This is what Hezekiah did throughout Judah, doing what was good and right and faithful before the Lord his God. In everything that he undertook in the service of God's temple and in obedience to the law and the commands, he sought his God and worked wholeheartedly. And so he prospered. (2 Chronicles 31:20–21)

Nice.

So the beginning of chapter 32 comes as a bit of a surprise. That old roller-coaster of faith takes another dip as yet more opposition kicks in. Even

Ezra (the prophet who we believe wrote 2 Chronicles under the inspiration of the Holy Spirit) sounds a bit amazed:

> After all that Hezekiah had so faithfully done, Sennacherib king of Assyria came and invaded Judah. He laid siege to the fortified cities, thinking to conquer them for himself. (2 Chronicles 32:1)

What a turn-up! Here's a guy giving it all he's got to serve the Lord. He's seeing real breakthrough and by all possible measures, he's doing well. Then the worst possible thing happens. OK, so there's every chance that there are a few years between the last verse of chapter 31 and the first of chapter 32 but still it must be said (as we'll see in more detail later) that as far as the Bible is concerned, God's definition of prosperity is probably slightly different from our own. Here, it simply doesn't equal peace or lack of opposition. In fact, every single man or woman of God down the history of the church could say amen to that. So can we too, if we've made up our minds to give all we can to Jesus.

When we decide to follow Jesus like this, there are two things that happen. First, we will get to know the smile of God on our lives, meaning that we'll be able to start seeing some of that godly fruit that's so important. Secondly, we will also find ourselves faced with surprising opposition and discouragement without God seeming to be there. By backing off for a bit, he is able to teach us some big lessons. There are other times when the enemy gets his big guns out to try and destroy us, but either way the real reward comes to the man or woman who holds fast to the Lord through all the hassle that goes with living on the cutting edge for Jesus.

You've probably noticed that heroes of the faith, both in the Bible and in church history, are a great inspiration to me. I love to hear about all those men and women who realised that they really did have a relay race marked out for them. They knew that while they had the baton in their hand it was their job to run as hard as they could to make Jesus known in their generation. It's so good to read about the way they stuck it out with

God and kept on moving forwards, no matter what the opposition.

William Carey was born in 1761. He's really the godfather of the modern missionary movement, who happened to be around at an interesting time. The church had been continually growing over the centuries but about 250 years ago things went nuts. The growth went into overdrive as God gave guys like William Carey a massive heart for the world. William was a cobbler and in his shop he had made a basic globe out of leather. While he repaired his customers' shoes he would look at the globe and pray and weep for the nations of the world that didn't know of Jesus. Wherever possible, he would challenge people and try to shake the church out of its apathy. As far as he could tell, people needed to get busy and fulfil Jesus' command to 'go and make disciples of all nations' (Matthew 28:19). He would often burst into tears as he shouted: 'The people living in these areas are pagans! They are lost, hundreds of millions of them, not knowing the blessed Saviour!'

There are no prizes for guessing that he was regularly put down and criticised. Once, a famous minister stood up at one of these meetings where William was ranting away. The minister interrupted William: 'Young man, sit down! When God wants to convert the heathen he will do it without you!' The press called him a maniac and nicknamed him the Consecrated Cobbler. But still he stuck to his message, reminding people of a world that needed Jesus and a people who ought to be sorting things out.

He preached his most famous sermon on the 30th May 1792. He chose Isaiah 54:2–3:

> Enlarge the place of your tent, stretch your tent curtains wide, do not hold back; lengthen your cords, strengthen your stakes. For you will spread out to the right and to the left; your descendants will dispossess nations and settle in their desolate cities.

He gave his sermon the clear title: 'Expect great things from God; attempt great things for God'. What a fantastic motto for any life. On the back of this message, things kicked into multiplication mode as two days later a group of guys who had been at the service formed the Baptist Missionary Society. Since then, it has sent missionaries to thousands of territories around the world with the good news, but back in 1793 they started with our man William. On the 13th June, William Carey and his mates headed for India, where they lived amazing lives of self-denial and faced ferocious opposition. They didn't even see a single convert for seven years. While they were out there, William's first wife became violently insane and then died. He married again but his second wife also died. They started to translate the Bible into Indian dialects and built a printing-press in order to distribute their translations, but the building burned down and three years' work literally went up in smoke. It was hardcore stuff but William was glued to the Lord. He was sure that this was where God wanted him. So he stuck at it. When the time came for him to pass on the baton, William Carey had overseen the birth of a dynamic church in India. With the help of his friends, he had been able to translate the Bible into 34 different languages. Like Hezekiah, he campaigned tirelessly and was instrumental in bringing about the abolition of pagan child sacrifices and the practice of burning living wives with their dead husbands on their funeral pyres.

One of the guys who picked up the baton was C. T. Studd. He was about as different from William Carey the cobbler as you could imagine. He was a member of the aristocracy who went to Eton college, surely the poshest school in Britain, and then onto Trinity College, Cambridge University. He was a brilliant sportsman and eventually captain of the England cricket team. He became a Christian at the age of 18, but for 6 years he lived the high life and didn't really practise his faith until he was 24. It was hearing the preacher D. L. Moody that got C. T. Studd to re-dedicate his life to Jesus. Shortly afterwards, he wrote in his diary:

I cannot tell you what joy it gave me to bring the first soul to the Lord Jesus Christ. I have tasted almost all the pleasures that this world can give ... but those were as nothing compared to the joy that the saving of that one soul gave me.

Within a few months, he and a few others were on their way to China as missionaries. When they arrived, they dressed, ate and lived like the poor Chinese they were trying to reach. No one would have guessed that he was a former captain of the England cricket team and a fully qualified member of the aristocracy. Shortly after arriving, he turned 25 and inherited a vast fortune from his father. After reading his Bible and praying, he decided to give it all away to Jesus. He was massively challenged by the story of the rich young man who walked away from Jesus because he wouldn't give up everything. I can imagine the jumping for joy that must have taken off in D. L. Moody's mission office, George Muller's orphanages and the Salvation Army mission to India. These places were all on the receiving end of cheques from C. T. Studd as he went ahead and surrendered all he had for Jesus.

C. T. Studd served in India through all sorts of hassles and hardships for ten years, until ill health forced him to return to England. Back home, he continued to recruit missionaries in the UK but couldn't bear the thought of not reaching the 'pagans' for Jesus himself. So, from 1900, he did another six-year stint pastoring a baby church, this time in India. Once again, ill health forced him home.

By now, God had given him a heart for Africa, so as soon as he thought he was well enough, he made moves to get involved in pioneering missionary work in Sudan. He was penniless; his doctor wouldn't pass him as fit enough, and the committee of businessmen who had agreed to support him withdrew their vital cash. But God had told him to go. His answer to the committee was: 'Gentlemen, God has called me to go, and I will go. I will blaze the trail, though my grave may only become a stepping-stone that younger men may follow.'

C. T. Studd did well in Africa. He faced plenty of opposition, lost most of his teeth, had several heart attacks and eventually died there 21 years later in 1931. The last word he spoke was: 'Hallelujah!' Just before he died, he wrote a letter reflecting on his life:

> As I believe I am now nearing my departure from this world, I have but a few things to rejoice in; they are these:
>
> 1. That God called me to China and I went in spite of utmost opposition from all my loved ones.
> 2. That I joyfully acted as Christ told that rich young man to act.
> 3. That I deliberately at the call of God, when alone on the Bibby liner in 1910, gave up my life for this work, which was to be henceforth not for the Sudan only, but for the whole unevangelised world.
>
> My only joys therefore are that when God has given me a work to do, I have not refused it.

What a buzz it must be for these amazing men to be in heaven now and see the black, brown and yellow faces pouring into glory. God has used the platform of their incredible faith and sacrifice to build his kingdom in India, China and Africa. What might be awaiting us? How about if we picked up the baton and decided to run hard for our generation? When we get to heaven, I promise that we'll be glad if we have stuck it out with God: it's then that we will fully realise that not one bit of giving, serving and sacrifice for Jesus is ever wasted. Even if we feel that we are running blind – in fact, *especially* when we feel that God is overshadowed by absence and opposition – it's time to keep on going. The good stuff is only just around the corner.

5

A SMILE WORTH CHASING

'He ... did not cease to follow him'

As well as practising the art of keeping going in the absence of God's smile, it's also important that we learn how to chase the smile itself. Hezekiah was up for this, and he managed to live a life that went in the right direction. He attracted the Lord's attention in such a remarkable way because of one simple fact: he was a follower. A Christian isn't primarily someone who reads the Bible, prays, goes to church and shares a faith; a Christian is someone who follows Jesus.

Jesus didn't ask people to sign up for an easy-life club; he told them to leave everything and follow him. In Luke 4:14, Jesus has been in the desert praying, fasting and generally scrapping with the devil for 40 days. The Bible says he came out of the desert in the 'power of the Spirit' which, oddly enough, is exactly where we need to be if we want to follow him. Just as the disciples got the gift of the Spirit after Jesus ascended into heaven, so do we need to get filled up and move out with God's power in order to make our lives count. Lots of Christians are actually filled with the Spirit in church – like the disciples were in the upper room a few days later – but as far as I can see, not too many of us are actually *moving* in the power of the Spirit. The disciples didn't just stay all warm and cosy in their holy huddle. Instead, they walked down a few steps from the upper room out into the streets to start preaching the good news. The result was impressive: 3,000 people became Christians, and a church was born. Lots of us are waiting in churches with all the other believers for the power to come. Sadly, the real action and the real power of the Spirit is waiting for us out there on the streets.

As Jesus started to let his actions be directed by the power of the Spirit, he became sure of his calling and also started looking for guys in whom he could invest. He needed a crew to whom he could pass on the baton after his death and resurrection. Considering the nature of the mission, these men needed to be something special. So it was odd that he chose such unlikely candidates while he was walking along the shores of Lake Galilee – for example, Simon and Andrew, two working-class fishermen, who were going about their job when Jesus said to them: 'Come, follow me ... and I will make you fishers of men.' You might have expected hot-headed Simon to tell Jesus to get lost, or perhaps a little worse, yet there must have been something compelling about the way Jesus said it. How come? Because we are told: '*At once* they left their nets and *followed* him' (Matthew 4:20, my italics).

A little further on, the three of them came across some of Simon's and Andrew's competition in the fishing business, two young brothers called James and John. They happened to work in their dad's fishing business, or at least they did until Jesus came along. As soon as he showed up, the pair *immediately* left their boat and their father, Zebedee (presumably with his mouth open), and *followed* Jesus (v. 22).

I like the 'at once' and 'immediately' in these verses. When Jesus calls us to do something, it is not the time to take a quiet month out to reflect. When God calls, it's time for us to get on with it at once, if not sooner, even if (like myself) it takes a few years to get where you need to be.

A little later on, we read in Mark 2 that Jesus went back out beside the lake and came across Levi. This was a bit of a change in strategy, as Levi was far away from the lower social group to which the fishermen belonged. He was the local mafia man, a tax collector, and as such one of the most despised men in Galilee. He collected rip-off taxes for the Romans from the poor, defenceless Jews, and made his living by creaming off as much as he could for himself. It's pretty clear that Levi was not the ideal candidate to gain interest in your new movement, but Jesus saw something in this guy and said to him – yes, you guessed it – 'Follow me' (Mark 2:14). Immediately, Levi left his tax-collector's booth and followed Jesus. Later that day, he invited all his mafia friends and dodgy dealers round to his house for a meal. The religious leaders were horrified but, of course, Jesus loved it and explained himself by saying: 'It is not the healthy who need a doctor, but the sick. I have not come to call the righteous, but sinners' (Mark 2:17). Two thousand years later, Jesus is still calling all sorts of messed up, undeserving sinners to follow him. Which is a relief.

This week, my brother Michael and his wife Sue set off in the footsteps of C. T. Studd. They're heading to Sudan, where they will work as missionaries. Mike and Sue both had top jobs in the teaching profession but they've handed in their notice and sold most of their possessions, even parting with their precious dog, Lucy. Right now, they're living out of a VW camper van as they wait to go to war-torn Sudan, where there will be no electricity or running water. Having said that, there will be literally millions of people desperately needing their help. That's what it means for Mike and Sue to follow Jesus. For us, it may not necessarily mean selling everything and moving location but it will almost certainly involve expending energy and resources to serve the lost, the poor and the hurting.

I'm convinced that if the church would only focus on those three things instead of falling out over different doctrines and practices then we'd get the job done a whole lot quicker. A few decades ago, a whole army of Christians got a dose of God's heart for the poor. The United Nations was drawing the world's attention to the plight of refugees, and, spontaneously, British Christians started sending money in to the Evangelical Alliance, asking them to pass the cash on to the Christians working around the world alongside these displaced people. By 1967, so much cash had come in, without anyone asking for it, that something major needed to be done. The Evangelical Alliance wasn't really known for relief work, but they put a man named George Hoffman in charge of setting something up. Known by those working on the project as The Evangelical Alliance Relief Fund, it eventually hit someone that it ought to be called TEARfund. And so it was, and still is. I believe God smiled that the evangelicals – the sort who were best known for their preaching and for trying to keep everything perfectly sound – were getting on with helping the poor. Thirty-seven years later, Tear Fund now dwarfs the EA and is one of the top five relief charities in the UK, raising and giving away tens of millions each year, caring for the poor in dozens of countries in the name of Jesus. What is extra good about the whole thing is that it is supported by the whole church: from the Catholics to the liberals to the evangelicals and chandelier-swinging charismatics. Why? Because they have forgotten about their differences and focused on Jesus' target – the poor.

It's a similar situation to when we've done our city-wide missions and focused on people who don't know Jesus. At those times, the church has united like never before. If you try getting churches from different streams and denominations together to plan and pray around things like worship, ministry, or gifts of the Spirit, then in my experience there is always a tendency for them to fall out. But if you focus on the poor and the lost, then there is a much better chance we will get on and work together so that the world can know that God loves them (see John 17:23). We may not agree on much, but we do agree that we are going to spend all eternity in heaven together, so it kind of makes sense to get as many people as possible to join us. There's no surprise to find out that this is one direction in which we can always find God's smile.

At the end of his time on earth, Jesus breathed on the disciples and said: 'As the Father has sent me, I am sending you ... Receive the Holy Spirit' (John 20:21–22). When he said this, I think Jesus might well have been remembering that time three years before when he went into the desert after being baptised by John. Through those forty days of fasting, prayer and searching out God's plan, he became convinced of his calling. He left the desert sure of what he was supposed to do; by coincidence (the kind of coincidence that always happens to people who are sent by God and are moving in the power of the Spirit), as he arrived back home it was his turn to teach in the synagogue. As if one tasty coincidence was not enough, there was another lined up: the set reading for the day was a wonderful passage from Isaiah, Hezekiah's mate:

> The Spirit of the Lord is on me, because he has anointed me to preach good news to the poor. He has sent me to proclaim freedom for the prisoners and recovery of sight for the blind, to release the oppressed, to proclaim the year of the Lord's favour. (Luke 4:18–19)

There was obviously something very special about the way Jesus read the words because Luke says: 'The eyes of everyone in the synagogue were fastened on him' (v. 20). All the children went quiet; all the women, for whom this was their weekly chance to catch up on the news, stared at Jesus as he sat down and delivered his stunning sermon. It might not have been the longest sermon they'd ever heard, but once those eight words were out of his mouth the world would never be the same again: 'Today this scripture is fulfilled in your hearing' (v. 21). For the next three years, Jesus went ahead and fulfilled that incredible prophecy. He preached good news to the poor; he proclaimed freedom for the prisoners; he restored the sight of the blind, and he released the oppressed. And then, on a hillside just before he ascended into heaven, he said something vital to all of us: 'Go on, follow me; it's your turn now. Here's my Spirit within so you can do just that.'

Christians down the centuries have argued about these verses in Matthew 28 and Mark 16. They've argued about whether the most important thing is that we preach the word, care for the poor or do great miracles. The answer is that following Jesus involves all three. Just preaching won't do it, unless we demonstrate it through kindness and miracles. On the other hand, lots of miracles and kindnesses are like 'dynamite without a detonator': if we don't preach good news alongside them, then the whole thing lacks that certain punch. One thing's for sure, if we aren't passionate and doing something sacrificial to reach out to the physically and spiritually poor, then we are almost certainly not following Jesus.

We live in a nutty world where around one billion people live on less than a dollar a day and three billion on less than two dollars a day. Despite all the advances in communication and travel, there are still literally billions (including millions on our doorstep) who know little or nothing of the love of Jesus. The poor and the lost are everywhere. It takes courage and gutsy determination to go to them as he leads.

I like the fact that the Bible says that Hezekiah 'did not cease to follow' the Lord (2 Kings 18:6). I know lots of Christians who at first go off like a train, working flat out for the lost and the poor, but sadly, as they supposedly 'mature', a bit of the zeal and passion goes out of them. To all intents and purposes, they stop following the Lord and allow their lives to become an endless round of meetings with the in-club, spending any spare time in front of the television or enjoying their possessions. Admittedly, there are a lot of pressures on us all these days: our society encourages us to work every hour that God sends, which makes it difficult to fit in a fulfilling family life. Sometimes we give in to the temptation to go with the flow; sometimes we just fall victim to old-fashioned opposition and pain. There are so many reasons why we can be tempted to take our eyes off the target and settle for the easy life, but how much better to be known when we are old as 'someone who didn't cease to follow the Lord'.

Hezekiah had all the excuses in the world to stop following God. If he'd felt that way inclined, he could have blamed any number of factors and ducked out of the race: a dysfunctional family background; the outrageously high levels of criticism and negativity that came his way; the attacks he endured when he was just trying to serve the Lord; the mistakes and dodgy decisions he made. As you'll probably be glad to know, Hezekiah wasn't perfect. As we'll see later in 2 Kings 20, we find him making a big mess of things and getting properly told off by Isaiah, but throughout it all he remained true to his beliefs, refusing to give up on chasing the smile of God.

It's nice that two of our Eden team workers share the names of Jesus' first two recruits. Manchester Simon and Manchester Andrew both have that passion and dedication that Galilee Simon and Galilee Andrew had, and they both make tough choices every day. Our Simon could easily have decided to give up on following Jesus at any number of points, like the time when the local gang burst into their church service with balaclavas and BB guns and started to shoot people. Then there was the time when he threw one of the local hooligans out of the youth club for violent behaviour. The lad ended up following Simon home, dowsing him with petrol and attempting to set fire to him. Thankfully, his lighter wasn't quite up to the job and Simon made it home in safety, but badly in need of a shower.

Andy, Simon's housemate, could also have chosen to quit when the local lads put dog filth through his letterbox. Or when they trashed his computer. Or when they cut the brake cables on his van. Or, worst of all, when Andy witnessed an attempted murder on his doorstep.

He saw it all, and was in a position to testify against this local, notorious gang leader. A few people had been in similar positions before, but, what with one thing or another, nobody had ever got up in the stand before. Andy felt convinced that the only thing he could do was to testify, even though it didn't seem like a very sensible option to take. The next day, he got six texts and emails from different people – three of whom didn't know about the situation – all with verses from Psalm 91 promising safety and protection from the Lord. If he had received these verses once, it would have been encouraging; twice would have definitely been the Lord, but six times is ridiculously God, and is the kind of thing that only seems to happen to people who really sacrifice and really need God to turn up.

Amazingly, when it came to the trial, there was no need for Andy to testify as the gang leader pleaded guilty and was sent down for 14 years. On the back of all this, the gang disbanded and their grip on the area has been pretty much broken. What is even more fantastic is that now, one by one, the lads who had bugged Andy's and Simon's life with all their dodgy deeds are finally getting acquainted with the smile of God for themselves. I love to hear the stories of them getting filled with the Spirit and crying out to God for their area in Andy's and Simon's front room.

Recently, I was at a meeting just before three of these lads got baptised. One of them, a guy named Jordan, who had been at the heart of much of the trouble for Andy and Simon, said: 'I don't want to disrespect Andy but I really believe it's us and all our mates that are going to see this area changed for Jesus. It's like the Eden workers have set the ball rolling.' I was so excited that I thought I might spontaneously combust!

Who knows whether these wonderful things would have happened if our latter-day Simon and Andrew had packed in all their God-following when the going got tough? In many ways, what they've done makes no sense at all. Getting involved in the mess and pain of inner-city Manchester, or the aftermath of war in Sudan, or wherever else you might go to care for the poor and the lost, just seems foolish to so many people. There you are, getting stuck into a mass of pain and sacrifice, but for what? If the others are right and there's no heaven, then all this work is pure madness. But there is a heaven; there is a God; there is a smile that comes out after the storm, the long night, or the trek through the desert. And when we get to heaven, it is only what has been done for Jesus that will count. Do you really want to give up on that yet?

Like my brother, C. T. Studd and thousands of others, a guy called Albert Schweitzer went to Africa as a missionary. He said that 'the only really happy people in the world are those who have learned to serve'. He's right. They've ditched the agenda set for them by society; they're not looking for happiness in possessions, status, or power. And despite all the difficult stuff they face, the truly weird thing is that Mike, Sue, Andy and

Simon are actually some of the happiest people I know. They've chased that smile of God down, through time, through pain, through sacrifice. Just one look at them is enough to know that it's worth every ounce of effort.

6

A Smile Worth the Price

*'He kept the commands the Lord
had given Moses'*

More than any other, this is the chapter I'm struggling to write. I know that in my Christian life to some extent I've put my faith to the test; I've stuck with it through some pretty stiff opposition and I've had a go at following Jesus to the poor and the lost. However, as I start to write about the holiness without which the Bible says 'no-one will see the Lord' (Hebrews

12:14), I'm feeling massively convicted. I know that I am not the man I should be. When it comes to purity and godliness, I'm in need of help. I also happen to know I'm in good company: probably the greatest Christian who has ever lived said: 'I have the desire to do what is good, but I cannot carry it out. For what I do is not the good I want to do; no, the evil I do not want to do – this I keep on doing' (Romans 7:18–19). Despite the encouragement of knowing that Paul struggled too, I look at the life of Hezekiah, as well as some of the other greats of history, and I so want to be better. I want God to know that I'm serious about him; I want to see him getting down to business in my life and work. But I know the truth, too: none of this will happen unless I make a commitment to being holy.

It really is the most extraordinary statement to be able to make about someone that they 'kept the commands the Lord had given Moses' (2 Kings 18:6). Hezekiah did, and the commandments given to Moses in Exodus 20 all those years ago are still the framework for any successful society and worthwhile life today. With the four instructions about our relationship with God and the other six explaining how we should relate to each other, the Ten Commandments set the standard for our behaviour. And if you check out the way that Jesus interpreted them in Matthew 5, it's soon clear that unless we have the power of the Spirit helping us, we're going to find it hard to come up to scratch.

I wonder if the writer of 2 Kings, as he scribbled these amazing words about Hezekiah, was thinking back to all the previous kings of Israel of whom it couldn't be said. Even golden boy David, perhaps the most famous of all the kings, broke the commandments one by one. He made a fantastic start, and was plucked out of obscurity at the age of 30 simply because God saw his heart. If ever a man had the smile of God on his life and knew the presence and prosperity of the Lord, it was David. It got even better as he found himself on a bit of a roll: reconquering Jerusalem; defeating the Philistines; bringing back the ark of the covenant, and leading the people into a fantastic period of peace and success. He must have appeared invincible, but there was one chink in his armour that would lead to a massive fall: he couldn't control his lust. This is the exact area in which I believe more men and women slip up than any other sin. Today, millions of Christians are facing serious temptation, and if they don't check it and stamp it out, it is bound to lead to a tragic fall like David's.

It's interesting that we can spy the first signs of David's fall well before it actually happened. In 2 Samuel 5 it mentions that 'David took more concubines and wives'. This may sound a bit weird today, but back then it was perfectly legal and socially acceptable for a king to have many wives and concubines. However, it wasn't on the menu for a man of God. Deuteronomy 17 sets down the standard for godly kings and commands them not to take many wives. But because handsome, charismatic David had a bit of a thing for the ladies, he wasn't listening and built up his harem against the will of God.

R. Kent Hughes, who wrote *The Disciplines of*

a Godly Man, said: 'It is the legal sensualities, the culturally acceptable indulgences that will drag us down.'[1] In other words, it is the stuff that others happily get away with that we need to watch out for: like indiscriminate watching of TV and films, regularly drinking that bit too much or going too far sexually outside marriage. These things are all perfectly legal and socially acceptable, but if we're up for pursuing holiness they are a clear no-no. When I was a brand-new Christian, I heard Ronald Dunn preach on 'Others can ... you can't'. It sounds a bit stiff, but actually it's an absolute key to knowing the smile of a holy God on our lives. Other people, even other Christians, may be able to justify stuff but that's not our problem. We are chasing after God, and because of that we know that there are things that others can do but that we cannot.

David gradually became desensitised to sin. Bit by bit, his standards got chipped away so that

---

[1] *Disciplines of a Godly Man* by R. Kent Hughes (Crossway, 2001), p. 23.

when he saw the gorgeous Bathsheba bathing provocatively below him, he didn't do what any sensible godly man would do – leg it – he stayed for an extended lech and made up his mind to find out who she was. Of course, finding out that she was the wife of one of his generals should have been an end to the matter, but lust had taken full control, as it so often does if we don't stop it at the first opportunity. So they had sex. I'm sure that if David had known where this little thrill was going to lead he would have run a mile, but he had become weak and lazy. What happened? A chain of events kicked off, and by the end of the affair she was pregnant; her husband had been murdered, and David was exposed to the masses as a sham.

What is really scary is that from this point on, even after David's total repentance and God's forgiveness in Psalm 51, it's as if everything is hard work. The smile, so it seems, is gone from his life. His baby dies; his daughter is raped; his son is murdered; his other son hates him so much for what he had done that he leads a rebellion against him – and all for a bit of nookie.

I've heard these words quoted many times. If only David had realised their truth:

- Sow a thought; reap an action.
- Sow an action; reap a habit.
- Sow a habit; reap a character.
- Sow a character; reap a destiny.

So there he was, the king who didn't keep the commands the Lord had given to Moses. He'd broken the seventh (do not commit adultery), the tenth (do not covet your neighbour's wife), the eighth (in stealing her) the sixth (in murdering Uriah), the ninth (in bearing false witness) and the fifth (in bringing dishonour to his parents) and, of course, in this way he also dishonoured God, totally breaking the first four commandments as well. What a mess!

I'm sure we'd all agree we don't want to end up like that, so what precautions can we put in place to ensure that our life doesn't go off the rails? How can we stay close to Jesus? The key word – as R. Kent Hughes would tell us – is discipline. It may sound boring and old-fashioned but having a disciplined life really is key to living it to the full. Disciplined prayer and Bible study, disciplined accountability groups are the best way to fend off the temptations that will surely come our way.

I'm a Manchester United fan and, while others may disagree, I'd say that the three most exciting players I have ever seen at Old Trafford over the past 30 years were David Beckham, Eric Cantona and George Best. It's interesting that I've heard Alex Ferguson, the United manager praise both Beckham and Cantona for being totally committed to their training. Day after day, they would both stay behind for hours practising their free kicks and their shots with the poor youth team goalkeeper. Then there was George Best – probably the best of the lot, but instead of staying back late he'd be the first one off down the pub as soon as possible after training. His glorious career was effectively over by the time he reached his mid-twenties, and an incredible talent was wasted. Let's make sure that we don't waste what God has invested in us by not putting in enough practice behind the scenes.

I also remember hearing an interview with the United Kingdom's only entrant in the Olympic weightlifting competition in 2000. I think he ended up in 14th position, and he certainly wasn't a household name, but he was making unbelievable sacrifices every day to be the best he could at his sport. He would be up at the crack of dawn to fit his training in with his work. His diet, his sleep patterns, his lack of friends, the financial, mental and emotional commitment, well they'd all obviously taken their toll on the poor guy. But when the interviewer asked him what he was planning on doing after the Olympics, the weightlifter answered: 'It's back to training. I intend to get a medal in four years' time.' Surely our pursuit of Jesus and his holiness should be just as passionate and committed, shouldn't it? It's just that instead of weights and carb counting, we need to do the business with the Bible, in prayer and with other Christians.

The other thing that will really help us in our walk with God is being disciplined about outreach. It was a year ago when this came home to me. I was feeling challenged that I was doing lots of spouting on the stage about evangelism but in my personal life things were slightly different. With several of my friends, we'd reached a sort of weird unspoken agreement where they all knew I was a Christian but they'd decided that it wasn't for them, and we could all be mates if we didn't let side issues like Andy's wacky faith mess things up. I knew God wasn't happy with this, and that I needed to do something about it. So, after discussing things with my vicar, we started a group at my house where we could have God-chats in the most informal way possible. I invited several of my friends and neighbours, and a few of the other people who had started showing up a bit at church but weren't yet Christians. It was a bit of a surprise when they turned up with several bottles of wine for the first session! But we had a great time eating and drinking and I've got to say that, including all the massive city-wide missions and gigs to thousands, it has become one of the most exciting things I have ever seen. To watch as one by one over the last few months they have been wooed by God has been fantastic. They come with bags full of problems – including marriages that are on the rocks and partners who have cancer, mental health and alcohol problems – but now, after lots of meetings and tons of times going out having a laugh together, we have a group of 15 or so going-for-it Christians who are starting to serve God in all sorts of ways.

Why am I telling you this? Because leading this group and helping to lead these cool people to Jesus has been a huge challenge to me to get the rest of my act together. These people know me well and see me close up; I've got to live right and be a good example. It's actually pretty easy to look holy in front of a crowd with a big Bible in your hand, but where it really counts is at home and in front of your mates. If we are going to stand up for Jesus in a godless world, it is massively import-ant that the people we work with, go to school with, or are friends with don't just know that we call ourselves Christians, but that we live it out loud as well.

A friend of mine called Wallace went to

university. When he arrived, he asked God to give him an opportunity to share his faith with some-one before the end of the first day. Sure enough, later on that day Wallace had a brilliant conversa-tion about Jesus with one of his fellow freshers. So he prayed the same prayer the next day and the next; in fact, he kept going for the whole three years that he was there. Every single day, he was able to talk positively to at least one person about the most important news in the world.

Things might be different for you. You might not find that all your friends come to Jesus, or that you have wonderful opportunities to share your faith openly wherever you go. People might misunderstand you or they might make fun of you. Fine. You know what you can do? You can hold on to the fantastic little verse that I always give to brand-new Christians: 'I tell you, whoever acknowledges me before men, the Son of Man will also acknowledge him before the angels of God' (Luke 12:8). Every time we make our stand for him, Jesus sees it and heaven knows about it.

For Hezekiah, responding in a godly way

meant digging deep and handing over serious sacrifices to God. The New Testament changes the plan a little: we no longer have to deal in animals to show our commitment to God; instead, we are being called to offer something much more costly. We must present our bodies 'as living sacrifices' (Romans 12:1). This is not easy. It is also not an optional extra. We have all been told to live a life of sacrifice, and these words come after eleven chapters of pure gold, in which we are given the greatest explanation of just how glorious the Christian faith can be. Paul explains the extravagant love of God towards sinners like us in great detail and then hits us with a 'therefore' at the start of chapter 12. Words like 'therefore' and 'but' are the hinges that Paul hangs his arguments on. My old youth leader used to say: 'If you ever see a "therefore" in the Bible, make sure you know what it's there for!' Well, this 'therefore' has a pretty clear purpose: we need to realise that because the gospel is so amazing, because Jesus' sacrifice was so costly, we ought to make our whole lives a sacrifice in return. Here it is:

Therefore, I urge you, brothers, in view of God's mercy, to offer your bodies as living sacrifices, holy and pleasing to God – this is your spiritual act of worship. Do not conform any longer to the pattern of this world, but be transformed by the renewing of your mind. (Romans 12:1–2)

Paul's message is not designed to help us get more out of Christianity. Instead, it is there to illustrate what we must do in response to God's fantastic mercies. Once we've understood just how extravagant God's love is towards us, we simply have to give him everything. John Stott put it like this: 'God's grace, far from encouraging or condoning sin, is the spring and also foundation of righteous conduct.' C. T. Studd also had something to add, famously saying: 'If Jesus Christ is God and died for me, then no sacrifice I can make can be too great.' They're both right, and one of the most challenging things Jesus himself said was: 'If anyone would come after me, he must deny himself and take up his cross and follow me' (Matthew 16:24).

My wife Michele works with our Eden project

in Salford, heading up their arts and crafts group. Last week, one of the young reprobates that the team have been trying to work with burst into the centre and stole lots of stuff, including Michele's purse. Within minutes, he had taken several hundred pounds out of her account. This is the second time she has lost her purse in the last couple of months, and both times we've had all the added hassle of cancelling cards, going overdrawn and all that stuff. When she got home and told me, I was furious and started ranting. 'I can't believe it,' I said, 'you just love and serve these guys and in return they treat you like crap.' Suddenly, I felt a bit bad and calmed down. 'I suppose that's not a bad description of how it was with Jesus.' I said.

In his book *Glory in the Church*, Jarrod Cooper tells the story of a zealous young worship leader who asked the Lord to show him what real worship is. I think he expected to see millions upon millions of angels singing: 'Holy, Holy, Holy is the Lord.' Instead, the picture God gave him was of:

.... an imprisoned man being strapped to a table. Once his arms and legs were locked in place, several guards took batons and began beating the soles of the man's feet, breaking his bones, ripping open the skin and smashing away his toes. The man's back arched and trembled with the pain as the guards screamed 'Deny him, deny him!' The man opened his mouth – the guards still beating his feet into a bloody pulp – and wailed 'I worship you my Jesus! I will not deny you! I thank you for your love and for your cross. I will praise you while I have breath!' God spoke into the heart of the young worship leader: 'That is worship.'[2]

Let's get this straight then: the business of being a living sacrifice is on the agenda for every one of us. It's as important a command for a student in Manchester as it is for a missionary in Sudan, or for our persecuted brothers in China. You want it plain and simple? We are God's people and we have to live differently and sacrificially. We're not

---

[2] *Glory in the Church* by Jarrod Cooper (Authentic, 2003), p. 55.

supposed to offer just a few hours each week or a bit of our money every now and then, but everything we have has to be given up as our act of worship.

This is tough, which is something that I find strangely comforting. But what confuses many of us is working out how actually to tell that we are serious about our faith. The answer is clear: it is by making sure that we do not 'conform any longer to the pattern of this world' but are 'transformed by the renewing' of our minds. We are all the subject of various influences, and you, today, are no exception. The question is whether the next 24 hours are going to see you becoming more worldly minded (with you getting closer to the centre of things) or more heavenly minded (with Jesus in his rightful place).

If we spend hours every day watching slightly dodgy TV programmes, reading iffy magazines and only spending a few minutes getting into the Bible and prayer, then there really isn't any wonder that we end up getting moulded by the patterns of the world. The more we worry about what we are like on the outside rather than on the inside, and the more we get off on instant highs, the more we are going to chase down earthly treasure instead of investing in that which has an eternal value.

I often look out at the crowds at the churches and conferences that I speak at and feel blown away by the unbelievable potential among them. If only we could all get serious about this business of being a holy and pleasing sacrifice. If only our worship could be lives laid down, rather than just songs sung in a moment's enthusiasm. There have been times at the end of these massive meetings when I've heard people complain that they 'didn't get much out of the worship'. This makes me sad: how far is this mind-set from the truth? How much more conformed to the pattern of the me-centred world could you get than to think that worship is about us getting stuff out of it? Worship is all about him. Sometimes it feels great but even when that happens it's largely irrelevant: what counts is that it's pleasing to him.

Real worship is about a lot more than singing

songs: it involves saying no to the sins that constantly trip us up; it means carving out time in our schedule for Bible study and prayer BEFORE we allocate time to the other 'essentials' that take up our time; it means finding some Christian mates we can be dead honest with who also want to be living sacrifices and who, together, can hold us accountable to the kind of life God wants us to live.

Right now, God isn't looking for dead sacrifices like Hezekiah's. He's interested in real, living, flesh-and-blood sacrifices. Yes, we may feel uncomfortable putting our lives on the line, but because the incredible good news of Jesus has gripped our hearts and lives so much, we're prepared to live a different way. God is after worshippers who are prepared to put up with criticism rather than honour, giving wealth and resources away rather than grabbing more for themselves, chasing after God's glory rather than their own pleasure.

Dietrich Bonhoeffer was one of the most remarkable men of the twentieth century, and he happened to chase God regardless of the price paid. He was a German pastor and theologian who had a passion for churches to work together. His most famous message was on Matthew 5 and what he called 'cheap grace': his major concern was that Christians were taking on a cheap grace rather than the costly grace of the New Testament. 'Real grace will cost a man his life,' he often said.

At the start of World War II, he had the opportunity to put these words into practice. While the majority of the Christians in Germany kept quiet as the vile Nazi regime tried to conquer the world and exterminate the Jews, Bonhoeffer spoke out on their behalf and became a leader in the part of the church that stood up to the Nazis. He reported the horrors of the war and spoke out against the prison camps. Inevitably, he ended up in a concentration camp in 1943, from where he wrote his famous prison letters. He was hanged in 1945, and the tree on which he died now has a plaque on which is written only ten words: 'Dietrich Bonhoeffer, a witness to Jesus Christ amongst his brethren.'

He once wrote that 'the cross is laid on every Christian – the first Christ-suffering which every man must experience is the call to abandon the attachments of this world. It is that dying of the old man which is the result of this encounter with Christ ... When Christ calls a man, he bids him come and die.'

Hard as they are, these words of one of the twentieth century's great martyrs definitely sum up how we are meant to be living if we really want to know the smile of God on our lives. They remind us that holiness and keeping the commands of the Lord do not involve living on a higher plane and floating around with a cheesy smile on our face. Instead, it's all about having a gutsy, hardcore discipline and determination to live differently through thick and thin, and stand out for Jesus in a messed-up world.

7

A Smile Through the Pain

'The Lord was with him; he was successful in whatever he undertook'

As we come to the end of this book, there's one big question that simply refuses to go away. Are you ready for it? Here goes: is God with us right now, making us successful in whatever we undertake? And of course there's another question queuing up behind it: just what would happen if the answer was yes?

We ought to want that 'yes' so badly. We ought

to be craving the chance to live by the very same principles that Hezekiah lived by all those years ago. But I'll be honest with you about it too: if it did happen, some of us might be a little bit surprised at what it looked like.

Let me explain. To have the Lord with us, and I mean *really* with us, has got to be what every Christian wants. To be at the heart of a major national revival which doesn't just fill churches but also transforms communities – just as it did for Hezekiah – has got to be good. How awe-inspiring would it be to have it said about us that, like the disciples, we have been with Jesus (see Acts 4:13)? How great an aim is it that we want to see our city or town filled with the teaching of Jesus? How exciting would it be if our dreams today become reality tomorrow? Well, that's exactly what happened to a bunch of people that were criticised by the religious big boys of the day. The elite rulers called the disciples 'unschooled' and 'ordinary', yet they experienced unprecedented presence and prosperity. Oh yes, then they got killed. One by one, they were butchered, stoned, thrown to the lions or crucified upside down. In all probability, there was only one of them that lived to see old age, and that was the exiled John. The Lord was with them big time; they were a huge success, but at what a cost.

Paul has got to be the most significant follower of Jesus out of the lot of them. He wrote about half of the New Testament, pioneered churches in nation after nation, and his life and words are still only beaten to the top of the pile by those of Jesus himself. Before he started getting serious with God, Paul was a political big boy, a man of influence and prominence. A few years later, after he had given his life over to Christ, he was treated like scum. How's that for weird?

In 2 Corinthians 11, he gives his testimony. Now this stuff is pure dynamite, and about as far removed from the kind of life story that gets trotted out by some of the shiny-toothed, white-suited evangelists of today. It goes like this:

Five times I received from the Jews the forty lashes minus one. Three times I was beaten with rods, once I was stoned, three times I was shipwrecked, I spent a night and a day in the open sea, I have been constantly on the move. I have been in danger from rivers, in danger from bandits, in danger from my own countrymen, in danger from Gentiles; in danger in the city, in danger in the country, in danger at sea; and in danger from false brothers. I have laboured and toiled and have often gone without sleep; I have known hunger and thirst and have often gone without food; I have been cold and naked. Besides everything else, I face daily the pressure of my concern for all the churches. (2 Corinthians 11:24–28)

How rough is that? The 'forty lashes minus one' was the beating Jesus received (think back to *The Passion of The Christ*, if you've seen that amazing film), and it alone was enough to kill you. The time he was stoned (presumably left with many broken bones), he was actually left for dead. His body must have been an absolute wreck, yet he called it all his 'light and momentary troubles' (2 Corinthians 4:17). Why? Because they were 'achieving for … [him] an eternal glory that far outweighs them all'. You see, Paul was truly successful because he was lost to this world; his heart was in heaven. In fact, he said: 'For to me, to live is Christ and to die is gain' (Philippians 1:21). In other words, he gave it all up, and then some. From the moment he met Jesus on that Damascus road, he knew he was going to heaven. As he got to know Jesus more, he was given some amazing revelations, of just how glorious heaven is. In 2 Corinthians 12:4, Paul says he was caught up into paradise and that he heard things so amazing that they were 'inexpressible'. What can you do to touch someone who has experienced something like that? If you kill them, it's just going to send them on to that amazing place a little sooner than they had expected. If you leave them alive, they can work hard to take as many people as possible with them. I pray that God will start to give us more and more people in this nation with that radical perspective.

I believe Paul was one of the richest men who ever lived. I'm not talking about having an exclusive pad in the hills of Jerusalem, or a shiny chariot on his drive: his wealth was far greater. He was a man who had learned the secret that eludes so many: the secret of contentment. As proof, he wrote these words to the church in Philippi:

> I know what it is to be in need, and I know what it is to have plenty. I have learned the secret of being content in any and every situation, whether well fed or hungry, whether living in plenty or in want. I can do everything through him who gives me strength. (Philippians 4:12–13)

On another occasion, he wrote that 'godliness with contentment is great gain' (1 Timothy 6:6). It's obvious that with contentment a poor man is rich and without it a rich man is poor. What's more, true contentment of the sort Paul is talking about can only come to the godly.

Right at the end of his life, he wrote this:

> I have fought the good fight, I have finished the race, I have kept the faith. Now there is in store for me the crown of righteousness, which the Lord, the righteous Judge, will award to me on that day – and

not only to me, but also to all who have longed for his appearing. (2 Timothy 4:7–8)

These are the words of a successful man whom the Lord has strongly supported. Wouldn't you like to be able to say something similar on your deathbed?

The first time I went to America, it was quite scary to hear a lot of stuff churned out by the Christian media. Every city seemed to have dozens of Christian TV and radio stations, and a lot of their output seemed to me incredibly man-centred. Instead of focusing on caring for the poor, the lost and the hurting, most of the teaching seemed to focus on stuff like how to sort out your finances, or how to be a success in business. Some of the more over-the-top channels definitely gave the impression that when God is blessing you, you'll always end up with a nicely swollen bank account. I even heard one smooth evangelist say: 'How can the world be driving round in Mercedes when the Christians have got Fords?' I nearly threw my shoe through the TV!

There's a serious problem here, a chronic misreading of the Bible. What these guys haven't properly thought through is that the vast majority of our brothers and sisters whom God is blessing massively, the ones whose faith totally puts us to shame, are actually poor. Or at least they are financially poor, but in my experience they are more often than not living with a godly contentment that is 'great gain'. Sometimes that's what is badly missing in our air-conditioned, high-tech Western churches.

So, being successful definitely doesn't mean getting rich. Hezekiah's story also shows that it doesn't mean avoiding mistakes either. The man made a few of them, one of the biggest ones happening when he foolishly tried to do a deal with his enemies. Instead of relying on God for strength, Hezekiah trusted in his own, which was a bit of a shame. Yes, the Assyrian army had been busily conquering one neighbouring country after another. Yes, they had just swept through Judah, ransacking dozens of towns and taking more than 200,000 captives, but was that a sign that Hezekiah should have started panicking? Of course not, but unfortunately he did. Instead of trusting in the Lord to deal with the Assyrians, he offered to 'pay whatever you demand of me' (2 Kings 18:14) if they would back off. In desperation, the king emptied the coffers of the Temple as well as the palace, even stripping the gold from the doors and doorposts.

Whenever we start playing games with our enemies (particularly the spiritual variety), the same thing starts to happen: we give them a taste and they soon return for more. The Assyrians did just that, and were soon threatening Hezekiah and his people, mocking the God of Israel and preparing for an all-out assault on Jerusalem. It was then that Hezekiah realised what a fool he'd been and cried out to God for forgiveness and deliverance. Despite his expensive mistake and all the pain that went with it, the Lord came through for him. The Assyrians received a terrible plague as 'the angel of the Lord went out and put to death a hundred and eighty-five thousand men in the Assyrian camp' (2 Kings 19:35). That's quite some counter-attack, and it's hardly surprising that the enemy quickly withdrew and left Jerusalem alone.

So if having God with us doesn't mean that we get rich, and it doesn't mean that we have a life free from attack, or even one where we don't make mistakes, then what does it mean? The answer's a short one: it means getting to know God and living a life that fulfils our God-given purpose. Paul said in Acts 20:24 (NLT): 'My life is worth nothing unless I use it for doing the work assigned me by the Lord Jesus.'

I hope that by reading this book you've taken on board that whoever you are, you really are designed for greatness. God has an assignment for you, and on the day that you became a Christian he signed you up to get on with the job of achieving it for him. Remember that Jesus said to you the day you gave your life to him: 'You did not choose me, but I chose you and appointed you to go and bear fruit – fruit that will last' (John 15:16). Jesus went right out of his way to choose you. Why? Because he loved you and because he believed in you. He didn't give you his Holy Spirit in order that he could lie dormant in you; he gave you his power so that you could do things you could never do in a million years on your own. It's those things of eternal importance that really count; they are the things that make people say: 'The Lord really is with this person.'

My brother and his wife have now arrived in Sudan. They're living in a little hut with a straw roof. In his first email, he wrote about being 'psyched' to be back in the developing world and mentions that 'a currency is one thing southern Sudan does not have of its own, along with no post, mains electrics, water, public transport and real ale! ... It is extremely interesting to live without these things.' He carries on like this for a while, until he comes to this line: 'Generally we feel very happy here; safe and at home and are confident that we are where God wants us to be.'

When I read this email, I spotted it straight away: a couple who, despite pretty much living in poverty without any of the things we think we need to make us happy, are living with the smile of God. The smile that comes from being 'confident' that they are where he wants them to be. In other words, fulfilling their unique God-given purpose.

As an evangelist, you can probably guess the kind of things I like to put up on my office wall. I've got a picture of probably the greatest evangelist of the lot: Billy Graham. He has preached face to face with more people than anyone in history, and underneath the picture is a quote of Billy's from years ago:

> My one purpose in life is to help people find a personal relationship with God, which, I believe comes through knowing Christ. I will never do anything as long as I live except preach the Gospel and I intend to do that as long as God gives me breath.

Billy Graham is now aged 86. He has advanced Parkinson's disease, a slowly worsening condition which causes disability and uncontrollable shaking, yet he has stuck to the words I look at on my wall. Last week, he preached to 80,000 people at a mission in Los Angeles, on the site of his first tent mission in 1949. He had to be brought to the stadium on an electric cart and raised to the stage on a hydraulic lift. He spoke from a pulpit that allowed him to sit if necessary because of injuries suffered earlier in the year when he fell twice and broke his pelvic bone in three places. Yet after his 45-minute talk, 13,000 people made a commitment to Christ. I'm confident that he was just as psyched as when he was a slightly brash, arm-waving young evangelist in the fifties. It's called being a man who has found your purpose, and it's one of the most precious things in the world.

Philip Yancey is one of the most significant Christian writers of recent years. In his stunning book *The Jesus I Never Knew*, he talks about his earlier work as a journalist, which gave him the chance to interview so-called stars, football greats, movie actors, pop stars and TV personalities. He puts it like this:

My career as a journalist has afforded me opportunities to interview 'stars', including NFL football greats, movie actors, music performers, best-selling authors, politicians and TV personalities. I have also spent time with people I call 'servants'. Doctors and nurses who work among the ultimate outcasts, leprosy patients in rural India. A Princeton graduate who runs a hotel for the homeless in Chicago. Health workers who have left high-paying jobs to serve in a backwater town of Mississippi. Relief workers in Somalia, Sudan, Ethiopia, Bangladesh, and other repositories of human suffering. The Ph.D.s I met in Arizona, who are now scattered throughout jungles of South America translating the Bible into obscure language.

I was prepared to honour and admire these servants, to hold them up as inspiring examples. I was not prepared to envy them. Yet as I now reflect on the two groups side by side, stars and servants, the servants clearly emerge as the favoured ones, the graced ones. Without question, I would rather spend time among the servants than among the stars: they possess qualities of depth and richness and even joy that I have not found elsewhere.

Servants work for low pay, long hours, and no applause, 'wasting' their talents and skills among the poor and uneducated. Somehow, though, in the process of losing their lives they find them.[1]

What a bizarre upside-down world we live in. I'm convinced that the reason these people are 'favoured' as Philip Yancey puts it is because they have found their purpose in life. They are fulfilling their destiny, and the God of heaven is smiling on their lives. I'm convinced that you and I can also know that same depth of richness and joy in our lives – we've just got to give it all over to Jesus and find out what good works he has planned in advance for us to do.

Please don't get me wrong: I'm not necessarily saying you must live among the poor to experience the smile. It's just essential that you find out what your part is in God's master plan as soon as you can. Pray, take advice, listen: it's the most valuable bit of knowledge you can ever pursue.

---

[1] *The Jesus I Never Knew* by Philip Yancey (Zondervan, 2003), p. 115.

For Hezekiah, it didn't mean living in a hut in Sudan but a palace in Jerusalem. Yet he managed to chase after God and in return received a burning passion for God's glory. He also received a strong desire to give generously from his own possessions (see 2 Chronicles 31:3) and to encourage the people constantly, even through the hard times: 2 Chronicles 30:22 explains that 'Hezekiah spoke encouragingly to all the Levites' and 32:6–7 says that even when faced with the Assyrian threats, Hezekiah 'encouraged' the people with these words:

> Be strong and courageous. Do not be afraid or discouraged because of the king of Assyria and the vast army with him, for there is a greater power with us than with him. With him is only the arm of flesh, but with us is the Lord our God to help us and to fight our battles.

There can only be one response to words as great as that: Come on!

As you ask God about just what he wants you to do with your life, you'll obviously be stocking up on prayer and advice. I reckon that there are a couple more things that will help you work things out too: First, give from your own possessions; don't wait until you've got a vast wad in the bank before you get into generosity. If you choose to wait until you're just over the next financial hurdle, you'll be waiting for ever. Instead, ask the Lord to get you excited about giving. Pretty soon, you'll find that you want to give more than just money, but time and effort as well. Before you know it, you'll be in the flow of serving him where you're meant to be. Second, I want to get you to be an encourager. In a world where lots of Christians who have so much to be thankful for spend an inordinate amount of time whingeing, encouragers are a major blessing. You can start today by looking for people who are struggling and telling them truths that will make them feel good about themselves. Look out for those kind and generous things people have done, and let them know you appreciate them. It's so easy to do and yet it means so much.

Wouldn't it be great to be known as someone

who 'refreshes the hearts of the saints'? Of course it would, especially when you bear in mind that it was precisely this type of behaviour that Paul valued so highly. It's not too hard to join the dots: God smiles on those who do his work.

I used to think that when people said to me: 'You are so tunnel vision!' and: 'All you think about is Manchester!' it was a criticism. Maybe it was sometimes. Still, these days I've decided to take that sort of stuff as a compliment. Short of a visitation from the Angel Gabriel, I believe that God has called me to this city for life. Until he changes the plan, I'm a firm believer that the race marked out for me – as well as for lots of others – involves playing our part in seeing this tough northern city turned round for Jesus. I know that nothing gets me 'psyched' like preaching the gospel and seeing Manchester's young people come to the faith. I also know that I sense the smile of God on my life when I'm dreaming dreams and stepping out in faith for this city. When I get to be an old man, I obviously hope I won't be on death row like Paul, but there are some similarities that I wouldn't mind sharing with the great man. I desperately hope that, like Paul, I'll be able to say: 'I have fought the good fight; I have finished the race; I have kept the faith. And along the way, the Lord has been with me and given me success in the things I undertook for him in this city.'

Hezekiah grew old and became terminally ill. It was looking as though the end was pretty close when God stepped in and healed him, handing out another 15 years of life. When it finally was his time to go, these special words are written of him:

> Hezekiah rested with his fathers and was buried on the hill where the tombs of David's descendants are. All Judah and the people of Jerusalem honoured him when he died. (2 Chronicles 32:33)

A few years before, he had taken over a nation that was in total chaos and disarray. Not only were they all tied up with the Baal religion but, probably as a result of these evil practices, they were socially and economically on their knees.

Over their heads was the permanent threat of invasion by the mighty Assyrian army, who were bit by bit conquering the Middle East. Every day that the Assyrians breathed was another day of threat and worry for God's people.

Once he was made king, Hezekiah made a wise decision. How about risking all on God? How about trusting him, following him, holding on tight to him and keeping his commandments? How about doing all that and seeing just what happens in this messed-up situation?

What happened? You know the script by now: the Lord was with him, and he was successful in whatever he undertook. God was put back on the agenda. A great revival broke out across Judah; the Assyrians were routed, and the nation was led into a period of tremendous peace and prosperity. Almost 3,000 years later, Hezekiah's life is still inspiring millions. Not bad for a guy whose dad was an absolute nutter!

A few years before, Ahaz had made a choice: he opted to indulge his appetites and ended up dealing with a whole load of destruction. He was booted out and 'not placed in the tombs of the kings of Israel' (2 Chronicles 28:27). Hezekiah chose another path, one marked by his decision to please and serve God. He 'rested with his fathers and was buried on the hill where the tombs of David's descendants are', having achieved all that could be hoped for and more. He died a glorious death; he had run his race; he had kept the faith, and there at the end, waiting for him after his death, was not the crown he'd worn as king of Israel but something far better: the crown of righteousness, which lasts for ever. It's a crown that is up for grabs by every true follower of God, a crown that one day you and I will receive. But there are some '*ifs*': if we give our lives to him; if we trust him; if we follow him; if we stick close to him, and if we give it our best shot at following his commands.

God's smile is a strange thing. It is there for all of us, one that is worth waiting for. We might not always see it, yet it is the only approval worth chasing. It is worth the price and – here's the shocker – the prize is unlike anything we could ever imagine. It has little status among the materialistic societies in which we lodge, but for those who get the closest to God's smile it even overpowers death itself. It won't make you rich. It won't make you free from failure. It's unlikely to make you live longer. But when you think about it, God's smile really is the only thing that counts.

Postscript

As I sign off this book, it strikes me that there may well be people reading it who aren't yet Christians. I would hate you to close the back page without sorting that out and making the most important decision you'll ever make.

As you've sussed out from these pages, becoming a Christian means making Jesus No.1 in your life and allowing him to control every decision you make about your future. It also means having a lot of extra help with your life as you start to live it out in step with his Spirit and begin to really squeeze the juice out of life. At the end of the day, he's God; he made you, and he's the only one who can show you how to live life to the full when you're here on earth, as well as how to get a life in heaven for eternity.

I know a lot of people who have become Christians, and all of them would say it is the best decision they have ever made. They'd also tell you that, hard as it is being a follower of Jesus, it's like the difference between living in black and white or colour. So, becoming a Christian is a massive world-changing decision, but in another sense it's as simple as ABC. All you have to do is:

Admit that you've let God down, done loads of stuff wrong and that you need forgiving.

Believe that Jesus was who he said he was – God come to earth – and that when he died on the cross, he was taking the rap for all the wrong things you've done. He rose from the dead, conquering death once and for all.

Consider if you are prepared to let go of the reins of your life and really make Jesus King. Being a real Christian will cost you time, energy and money. But in return you'll get the fullest life now and eternal life when you die.

If you've got this far and are still up for it, there is only one thing left to say:

Do it. Don't mess about. Go for it. You are not a Christian because you've read Christian books and know the facts about Christianity. You are a Christian because you've started a relationship with Jesus. You can start that relationship with a simple prayer like this one. Why not find a quiet place and make this prayer your own?

> Lord Jesus, I know I've done lots of things wrong. I know I don't deserve to go to heaven. I'm truly sorry, and I turn away from everything that I know is wrong in my life. Thank you so much for dying in my place. Thank you that you rose again and conquered death once and for all. Please fill me with your Holy Spirit. With your help I'll live all out for you for the rest of my life. Amen.

If you sincerely prayed that prayer, then you have just started a new life with Jesus in charge. He said: 'Whoever comes to me, I will never drive away' (John 6:37), so you can be sure that he's accepted you and that you are going to heaven in a few years' time. Until you get there, you can enjoy the privilege of every day trusting God, following him, sticking with him and obeying his commands. Go for it.

I'd love to send you (free of charge) a little booklet I've written about going on as a Christian, and a bit of the Bible. Just write to me at:

Andy Hawthorne
The Message Trust
PO Box 151
Manchester
M22 4YY
Or email me at andyh@message.org.uk

THE MESSAGE TRUST

The Message Trust has grown phenomenally over the past few years and we have a vision to see every young person in Greater Manchester presented repeatedly and relevantly with the good news and for all those that respond being given the chance to grow into all that God wants them to be in lively, Jesus-filled, local churches.

If you like the sound of that and could pray for us, give financially to help us do what we do or even consider joining us on an inner-city Eden project or our 5-month residential, training programme 'Genetik', then please contact us at:

The Message Trust
PO Box 151
Manchester
M22 4YY

T: 0161 946 2300
F: 0161 946 2310
Email: info@message.org.uk
www.message.org.uk